RESOURCE BOOKS FOR TEACHE

s

ALAN MA

LITERATURE

Alan Duff &
Alan Maley

Oxford University Press

Oxford University Press
Walton Street, Oxford OX2 6DP

*Oxford New York Toronto Madrid
Delhi Bombay Calcutta Madras Karachi
Kuala Lumpur Singapore Hong Kong Tokyo
Nairobi Dar es Salaam Cape Town
Melbourne Auckland*

and associated companies in
Berlin Ibadan

Oxford and *Oxford English* are trade marks
of Oxford University Press

ISBN 0 19 437094 1

© Oxford University Press 1990

First published 1990
Fourth impression 1992

Set by Pentacor Ltd, High Wycombe, Bucks

Printed in Hong Kong.

Acknowledgements

Many people have helped, in different ways, to shape this book. We should like to thank, in particular, the following:

Usha Aroor (Orient Longman, Madras), Peter Brown (The British School, Trieste), Nancy Campbell, Andrea Eschner, Harold Fish, Sue O'Connell, Bob Ness, Andrej Novak, Andrew Skinner, Michael Swan, Susan Leather (a special word of gratitude for invaluable help when it was most needed), and the many teachers and students who have tried out this material.

The publishers would like to thank the following for their permission to use copyright material:

Black Sparrow Press (for the poem 'This Subway Station', copyright © 1977 Marie Syrkin Reznikoff, from *Poems 1918–1975: The Complete Poems of Charles Reznikoff)*; Bloodaxe Books Ltd (for the poem 'Nightshift Workers', by George Charlton, Bloodaxe Books, 1989); Jonathan Cape Ltd and Jonathan Clowes Ltd (for *Mr Wrong*, copyright © 1975 by Elizabeth Jane Howard. Reprinted by permission of Jonathan Clowes Ltd, London, on behalf of Elizabeth Jane Howard); William Collins Sons and Co Ltd and Elaine Green Ltd (for *Sweet Dreams*, copyright © 1973 by Michael Frayn); John Ezard (for his article 'The Long Climb Back to Glory', in *The Guardian*); Faber and Faber Ltd and Harcourt Brace Jovanovich Inc (for *The Spire*, copyright © 1964 by William Golding); Faber and Faber Ltd (for *Skirmishes*, by Catherine Hayes); Harper & Row Publishers, Inc (for excerpts from *The Grass is Singing* by Doris Lessing. © 1950/1978 by Doris Lessing); Hamish Hamilton Ltd and Aitken and Stone Ltd (for *The London Embassy*, and 'Subterranean Gothic' from *Sunrise with Seamonsters*, by Paul Theroux 1985 © Cape Cod Scriveners Co); William Heinemann Ltd and Doubleday (for *The Moon and Sixpence*, copyright © 1919 by W Somerset Maugham); William Heinemann Ltd and A P Watt (for *The Human Element*, by W Somerset Maugham); William Heinemann Ltd and William Morrow and Co Inc (for *The Jewel in the Crown*, © 1966 by Paul Scott); David Higham Associates Ltd and The Putnam Publishing Group (for *The Spy Who Came in from the Cold*, by John Le Carré, copyright © 1963 Victor Gollancz Ltd); David Higham Associates Ltd (for *The Girls of Slender Means* by Muriel Spark, Macmillan); David A Hill (for his poem 'The Lesson', from *The Eagles and the Sun*, Prosveta, Nis. 1986); The Hogarth Press (for *Cider with Rosie*, by Laurie Lee); *The Independent* (for the article 'Police plan new strategy to make the Tube safer', by Terry Kirby and 'How Big Brother keeps trouble off the Clockwork Orange'); the estate of Christopher Isherwood (for *Goodbye to Berlin*); Alan Jackson (for his poem 'Goldfish'); Michael Joseph Ltd (for the poem 'Mabel', from *The Collected Poems of Stevie Smith*, Penguin Modern Classics); Macmillan Publishing Co (for the poem 'Memory', copyright © 1919 Macmillan, copyright renewed © 1947 Bertha Georgie Yeats, and 'The Second Coming', copyright © 1924 Macmillan, copyright renewed © 1952 by Bertha Georgie Yeats, from *The Poems of W B Yeats* ed. R J Finneran); Ellen C Masters (for the poem 'Silence', from *Songs and Satires* (Macmillan), copyright renewed 1944 by Edgar Lee Masters); Methuen Drama (for *Educating Rita* by Willy Russell); Penguin Books Ltd (for *The Penguin Guide to Ancient Egypt* copyright © by William J Murnane, 1983); Peters Fraser and Dunlop Group Ltd on behalf of the author (for poems by Roger McGough: 'Storm' from *After the Merrymaking* and 'Discretion' from *Watchwords* (both Jonathan Cape), and 'My Busconductor' from *Modern Poets 10 – The Mersey Sound*, Penguin Books); Peters Fraser and Dunlop Group Ltd and George Weidenfeld and Nicholson Ltd (for *Clinging to the Wreckage* by John Mortimer); Peters Fraser and Dunlop and Sterling Lord Literistic Inc (for *Rumpole of the Bailey*, Penguin Books 1978, copyright © by John Mortimer); Peters, Fraser and Dunlop Group Ltd (for *Labels* by Evelyn Waugh, Gerald Duckworth and Co); Poetry Wales Press Ltd (for the poem 'Cathedral Builders' by John Ormond); Laurence Pollinger Ltd and International Creative Management Inc (for 'Mortmain' from *Collected Stories* by Graham Greene, William Heinemann and

The Bodley Head); Laurence Pollinger Ltd and the estate of Mrs Frieda Lawrence Ravagli (for the poems 'After the Opera' and 'The Mosquito' from *The Collected Poems of D H Lawrence*, and *The Lovely Lady*, *The Fox*, and *Aaron's Rod* by D H Lawrence); Murray Pollinger and Alfred P Knofp Inc (for 'Poison' and 'Taste' by Roald Dahl, from *Someone Like You*, Michael Joseph and Penguin Books); Rogers, Coleridge and White Ltd (for the poem 'The Lesson' by Edward Lucie-Smith, from *A Tropical Childhood and Other Poems*, Oxford University Press 1961); Anthony Sheil Associates Ltd (for *The French Lieutenant's Woman*, © by John Fowles, first published by Jonathan Cape); Michael Swan (for his poems 'Nothing to Eat' and 'Girls in Airports'); Poseidon Press and A P Watt on behalf of the author (for *Learning to Swim*, © 1982 by Graham Swift); George Weidenfeld and Nicholson Ltd (for *A Summer Birdcage* by Margaret Drabble); Mrs Catherine Woods (for her poem 'Widowhood').

The publisher would also like to thank the following for their permission to use appeal and publicity material, and to reproduce artwork:

The London Transport Museum (for a poster from the series 'Poems on the Underground').

The Publisher has been unable to trace the copyright holders of the following, and would like to hear from them:

The poem 'Wasp' by Verity Bargate, and the US copyright holders only for *Goodbye to Berlin* by Christopher Isherwood and *Learning to Swim* by Graham Swift.

The publishers would like to thank the following for their permission to reproduce photographs:

Barnabys/J M Brown/J Chamberlain/P Lassen/B Michael/N Price/Reitz BTA
Britain on View
J Allan Cash Photo Library
Zoe Dominic Photo Library
Ann Hunter
Rob Judges
London Transport Museum
Mark Mason
Paul Rasmussen
Science Museum, London
Terry Williams

Illustration by: Bob Moulder

The publishers have made every effort to contact the copyright holders of photographs used in the book, but in some cases they have been unable to trace them. If the copyright holders of these photographs would like to contact the publishers, the publishers would be happy to pay an appropriate reproduction fee, and to arrange for them to be credited in any future reprints.

Contents

The authors and series editor

Alan Duff is a freelance writer and translator. He has also worked as a university lecturer in Yugoslavia, and as assistant English Language Officer for The British Council in Paris. As a visiting lecturer, he has worked in a number of countries including India, China, Hungary, Austria, Yugoslavia, and France.

In addition to the books he has co-authored with Alan Maley (see below), he has also written *That's Life!*, *The Third Language* (on translation into English), and *Translation*, which appears in this series.

His other writings include numerous short stories, as well as translations of plays, novels, and films. He has recently completed a series of programmes for the BBC World Service, *English by Radio*, entitled 'Tiger's Eye'.

The author has degrees in philosophy and literature.

Alan Maley worked for The British Council from 1962–1988, serving as English Language Officer in Yugoslavia, Ghana, Italy, France, and China, and as Regional Representative for The British Council in South India (Madras). He is currently Director-General of the Bell Educational Trust, Cambridge.

He wrote *Quartet* (with Françoise Grellet and Wim Welsing, OUP 1982). He has also written *Beyond Words*, *Sounds Interesting*, *Sounds Intriguing*, *Words*, *Variations on a Theme*, and *Drama Techniques in Language Learning* (all with Alan Duff), *The Mind's Eye* (with Françoise Grellet and Alan Duff), and *Learning to Listen* and *Poem into Poem* (with Sandra Moulding). He is also Series Editor for this series, the New Perspectives Series, and for the Oxford Supplementary Skills series.

Foreword

The role of literature in language teaching has been variously interpreted over the past 100 years.

In an earlier period, when the grammar-translation model was paramount, literary texts were the very staple of foreign language teaching, representing both models of good writing and illustrations of the grammatical rules of the language.

During the period of structural dominance, literature found itself side-lined. The formal properties of the language took precedence, and literature study was seen as part of the bad old 'traditional' methods. It was, moreover, difficult to justify the use of literary texts in a world where the grading of vocabulary and structures was given so much emphasis.

For a time the new functional-notional communicative movement also ignored literature. The emphasis was on pragmatic, efficient communication with no frills. Literature seemed like an irrelevance.

Yet in the last five years or so there has been a remarkable revival of interest in literature as one of the resources available for language learning.

This book is an attempt to explore further the use of literary texts as a language teaching resource rather than as an object of literary study as such. For, if indeed literature is back, it is back wearing different clothing.

The twin aims of the activities proposed in this book are to encourage the student to give close and repeated attention to the text and, at the same time, to interact with others about it.

Literature should prove of value to teacher trainers, practising teachers, and teachers in training who are interested in regaining access to the rich resource which literary texts offer.

Alan Maley

Introduction

Who is this book for?

Like the other titles in the Resource Books for Teachers series *Literature* is intended both for practising teachers of EFL/ESL and for teachers in training. Those preparing for the RSA Certificate or the RSA Diploma should find useful ideas in it.

Literature aims to provide a source of ready-to-use classroom materials for teachers working with young adult learners at a number of levels, including the Cambridge FCE and CPE examinations. However, it is not intended as a preparatory course in literature but rather as a set of interactive language materials based on literary texts.

What is the approach?

We must begin by removing one major potential misunderstanding. It is *not* our intention in this book to teach students how to study literature – either from the literary critical or the stylistics viewpoint.

The primary aim of our approach is quite simply to use literary texts as a resource (and it will not be the only resource) for stimulating language activities. This enables us to cut away the dead weight of critical commentary, metalanguage, and explanation which has historically been associated with work on literary texts.

What we are interested in is engaging the students interactively with the text, with fellow students, and with the teacher in the performance of tasks involving literary texts. In so doing, students are obliged to pay careful attention to the text itself and to generate language in the process of completing the task. Any enhanced understanding or literary insight which students may acquire as spin-off from this approach we regard as a bonus.

The following guidelines have emerged in the course of our work:

a. Of central importance is the text itself, not commentary or background information *about* the text. This may (or may not) be supplied later if the students express interest.

b. The student is an active agent not a passive recipient. It is vital for us that the activities provoke a genuine interaction between the reader and the text (preferably sending him or her continually back to it to check and re-check), and between the readers themselves – including the teacher!

c. The activities should offer ample opportunities for the students to contribute and share their own experiences, perceptions, and opinions. By their very nature literary texts give access to the worlds of personal experience which every student carries within.

d. The text should be allowed to suggest the type of activity. This means breaking away from the stereotypical format of text and questions. In many of these activities there are no questions at all, yet the task cannot be completed unless the text has been understood.

e. Texts can be presented in a variety of ways. This may sometimes mean withholding the text until the end of an activity, cutting it up, using fragments of it only, and so on. Texts may also be presented in fresh contexts by juxtaposition with other texts or media, or made to serve purposes for which they were not originally intended.

f. The text is not the only element in the activity. We regard it simply as one key element in a linked set of activities, which may include preliminary discussion, interactive work involving the text, and some sort of follow-up, often in writing.

g. Literary quality is not the only criterion for the selection of texts. Quite often 'bad' writing proves more useful or stimulating than 'good'. These texts are not necessarily presented as models of good writing. Students are not required to approve of them, but simply to work with them.

Why literature?

Essentially there are three types of justification for using literary texts: linguistic, methodological, and motivational.

a. In terms of the language, literary texts offer genuine samples of a very wide range of styles, registers, and text-types at many levels of difficulty. For this reason alone they are worthy of consideration.

b. The fact that literary texts are, by their very essence, open to multiple interpretation means that only rarely will two readers' understanding of or reaction to a given text be identical. This ready-made opinion gap between one individual's interpretation and another's can be bridged by genuine interaction.

c. Literary texts are non-trivial in the sense that they deal with matters which concerned the writer enough to make him or her write about them. In this they are unlike many other forms of language teaching inputs, which frequently trivialize experience in the service of pedagogy. This 'genuine feel' of literary texts is a powerful motivator, especially when allied to the fact that literary texts so often touch on themes to which learners can bring a personal response from their own experience.

What about 'difficulty' and 'level'?

What do we mean by 'difficulty'? Clearly the notion comprises a number of different aspects in regard to literary texts:

Linguistic difficulty

This may refer to syntactic complexity, lexical density, or discoursal organizaton.

Difficulty arising from text length

For some, longer texts will appear more difficult. For others, shorter texts present more difficulties simply because they do not offer the extended contextual support and repetition which longer texts do.

Cultural difficulty

This is notoriously difficult to define, though much has been made of it in recent years. To the extent that it is clearly impossible for the 'outsider' to share fully the range of references of an 'insider', cultural factors do offer difficulties. But to claim that nothing can therefore be got from a text by an outsider is patent nonsense. Lecturers (not students!) in India used often to observe that Wordsworth's 'Daffodils' could not be appreciated by Indian students because they had no direct experience of this exotic bloom. Taken to its logical conclusion this view could effectively preclude British readers from reading Commonwealth writing in English or indeed any works in translation. While problems clearly may arise, it seems to us that a better approach is to use these opportunities for exploration, rather than refusing to undertake the journey.

Difficulties of range of reference

These are related to cultural difficulties. They are best exemplified by works such as 'The Waste Land' which cannot be fully appreciated without the notes. But all literary works make reference to things outside themselves and are thus liable to misinterpretation, or to variable interpretation. This is one of the things which makes them interesting!

Conceptual difficulty

This refers to the difficulty of the ideas the text conveys, even when couched in simple, limpid language. William Blake's poetry provides good examples of deceptively 'simple' writing.

Acceptance difficulties

This has to do with the almost instinctive negative reaction we experience towards certain types of text or certain authors ('I can't stand detective stories.' 'I hate all those pretentious pseuds that Iris Murdoch writes about.'). So 'difficulty' is not at all a unidimensional problem.

Given that some or all of the above factors may render the text more or less acceptable for use in language learning activities, what can we do about it?

In the first place we need to accept that 'difficulty' is a subjective and relative matter. Different readers will find the same text more or less difficult. We can turn this to account in our activities by providing opportunities for information exchange among students.

If a text is 'too difficult' it should not be chosen. It would be foolish to choose texts which we know our students will not be able to cope with. There is such a wide variety of literary texts available that we can relatively easily operate a kind of intuitive grading, without actually tampering with the texts in any way. Although our selection of texts does not include much classical literature, this by no means suggests that we are turning our backs on 'traditional' literature. Our reasons for not including the classics are that they are more readily available than some of the texts we have chosen, and, in many cases, the literature of our times is more accessible to foreign learners. The activities described in this book can, of course, be adapted for use with set texts and other literary material.

If we do wish to use challenging texts, we can ease our students' approach to them by grading the activities or tasks. The range of activities in this book offers teachers a fair variety of different levels of demand.

One way of gradually building up the degree of demand on students could be:

Level 1 'Easy' text + low level task
Level 2 'Easy' text + higher level task
Level 3 'Difficult' text + low level task
Level 4 'Difficult' text + higher level task

For many teachers the issue of vocabulary load is the main constituent of 'difficulty' in literary texts. If, notwithstanding the points made above, there remain problems with individual words which continue to block understanding or the performance of the task, the teacher has available the same range of inferential techniques as for non-literary texts.

In brief, we feel that the issue of 'difficulty' in regard to literary texts can be exaggerated. It is likely that those who raise it as a warning spectre have in mind their own earlier struggles with literary texts in a foreign language (or even in the mother tongue).

But such texts were (and still are) chosen by virtue of their respectability as part of a literary canon in the context of the 'Study of Literature', not for language teaching purposes. This is precisely *not* what we are advocating. In our approach you, the teacher, are free to choose the texts.

But what about 'real' literature?

It is possible that some readers may feel that the approach we are advocating is reprehensible, even sacrilegious, because we do not seem to be taking literature 'seriously'. In addition, we might be seen as failing in our responsibility to teach 'real' literature, by which is generally meant a body of texts recognized as great literature, together with the procedures approved for studying it.

Let us simply make a number of points which hopefully go some way to meeting these objections:

a. We have made it very clear what our approach is. It is *not* the study of literature. To object that we have failed to do something we did not set out to do would be perverse.

b. There is nothing sacred about a literary text. All such texts were at some time written down, rearranged, scratched out, torn up, revised, misprinted, and so on. Anyone doubting this should simply look at any well-known writer's notebook or manuscript. The recently revised edition of Joyce's *Ulysses* is a good example of our literary conditioning receiving a rude shock!

More importantly perhaps, if students are encouraged to adopt a 'hands on' approach to texts, they are likely to lose some of the awesome respect which the printed word, and especially the literary printed word, inspires, and which gets in the way of the individual reader/interpreter's personal response to the text.

c. Our major interest is in the use of literary texts for language learning. Anything we choose to do with them which helps to achieve this purpose, is for us valid. It also helps to explain why we have not gone into techniques for the study of complete works of fiction or in-depth analysis of texts, both of which belong to the traditional *study* of literature.

d. We believe that our approach can be helpful even to those students who will eventually wish to study literature, since most of the activities deal with choice in one form or another: Why this word and not that? Why this order and not that? Why this format or length and not that? Why this piece of information and not that? Why this style and not that?

These are precisely the kinds of choices which writers themselves continually face. By taking students behind the scenes and giving them the experience of making choices of the same kind, we believe their subsequent understanding of literary processes can be increased.

We feel that by directing students' activities towards concrete rather than abstract speculation, they will find it easier to approach texts from a 'study' angle. One of the problems about more traditional approaches to teaching literature was the way students were encouraged to use a kind of Lego-metalanguage ('poetic sensibility', 'touching', 'trite', 'expressive', 'evocative', and so on). One does not need to 'speak literature' in order to talk about it.

This is why, in the activities, students are encouraged to say what they think in their own words, and to back up their opinions by direct references to the text.

We hope that *Literature* will provide ideas and procedures that will enable and encourage teachers to generate their own materials. The Appendix has been specially written with this in mind. We would also welcome comments on the ideas presented here, and information from any teachers who have developed further ideas and techniques. Correspondence may be addressed to us c/o Oxford University Press.

How to use this book

How the book is organized

Literature is divided into four sections of roughly equal length. These are:

1 **Starting-points**
2 **General approaches**
3 **Developing ideas: themes, topics, and projects**
4 **Over to you: further ideas, with a focus on language**

Section 1, *Starting-points*, introduces a selection of activities which can be used with students at most levels (including even native speakers!), and which do not require any formal knowledge of literature. The activities are designed to:

a. awaken interest: guessing, speculation, and discussion are encouraged
b. accustom students to working on short texts
c. introduce approaches that will later be used again with longer texts
d. provide you, the teacher, with material that is easy to prepare, adapt, and renew.

But above all our aim is to suggest starting-points – often non-traditional ones – which will lead to further discoveries.

In Section 2, *General approaches*, the emphasis is on activities which can be used with materials from very different sources. This means that the activities are not text-bound: you could use the same approaches with materials of your own choice. In addition to offering general strategies for approaching literary texts, we also suggest ways of dealing with longer texts such as short stories or chapters from novels.

Section 3, *Developing ideas*, concentrates primarily on discussion topics. Various themes, such as difficult jobs and childhood memories, are explored through the use of literary (and non-fictional) texts. One of the main aims of these activities is to give the students an opportunity to speak from personal experience.

Finally, in Section 4, *Over to you*, we consider further ideas, with a particular focus on language. Here, you will find suggestions for activities based on literary texts, which can be directed towards the improvement of a specific skill such as listening, or towards practice in a particular area of language. Our aim in this section is to suggest approaches which you could easily develop – and, of course, improve upon!

The book concludes with an *Appendix* which offers ten generative procedures for developing language activities. The procedures are described in detail, but the choice of content, that is, the literary material itself, is left to the individual teacher.

How each activity is organized

Each numbered activity is presented under five main headings: *Level, Time, Preparation, In class,* and *Notes.*

Level
This indicates the minimum level at which the activity can be carried out. Sometimes a range of levels is given to show that, with suitably adapted materials, the activity can be used with different levels.

Time
This is a rough guide to the amount of time the activity will take in class.

Preparation
This tells you what kind of preparation and/or materials you will need.

In class
Under this heading you will find a step-by-step guide to carrying out the activity in the classroom. Also included under *In class* are warm-up and follow-up tasks, as well as variations on the approach or the texts used in the activity.

Notes
The *Notes* are there to help you and your students to understand the purpose of the activity, to provide you with useful tips, and to point out some of the problems that might arise.

Ways of using the materials

1 Using the materials as they are

If you decide to use the materials as they are, without adaptation, you will need to exercise considerable judgement as to the suitability of any given activity for any given class. The book is emphatically *not* planned as a course, so it should not be worked through sequentially from beginning to end.

2 Incorporating the materials into your own course

If you have a free hand to build your own course, using materials from a variety of sources in a modular fashion, these activities can be incorporated in whatever proportion seems appropriate. Clearly, for most types of learner, they would only be one among many other types of language resource.

3 Integrating the materials into set coursework

If you are tied to a course book, we should suggest a modest, occasional use of carefully chosen activities, possibly starting with those likely to be familiar to students (for example, gap-filling). If this works well, it would then be worth analysing the course book in order to identify points at which particular activities from this book could be slotted in – either for linguistic or thematic reasons. The activities we propose here could then be integrated into the course book in a more or less systematic way. Indeed some of our techniques could be applied to the texts in the course book.

4 Using the book as a resource for ideas

If you decide to use the book as a resource for ideas, rather than as a source of immediately usable materials, you might still care to try a representative sample of the actual materials here before designing your own. This will give you a feel for the kinds of activity which succeed best with particular groups of learners. You will then need to research texts at an appropriate level of difficulty on which to apply the procedures you have decided to use.

We strongly recommend that you read the Appendix with care. In it we have tried to set out some basic underlying types of procedure from which you will be able to generate your own activities.

1 Starting-points

Introduction

The purpose of this section is to prepare the ground for using literature in the language class. Our main aims are:

1 To provide you, the teacher, with short, easy-to-follow activities which can be used even with classes which have no previous experience of working with literature.

2 To offer alternatives to the standard question-and-answer approach to texts. And, through these alternative approaches, to touch on questions such as: What do we think literature is? Is it only 'good' writing? Is it only fiction?

3 To encourage students to feel free with the texts, to comment, speculate, criticize and, above all, to offer suggestions.

4 To illustrate approaches which can be used with a variety of texts, and which can be adapted or expanded for use in longer activities.

It must be stressed from the start that these activities are designed specifically for language practice, not for literature study, although this does not mean that they would be of no value in the literature class. We emphasize this point because many students and, indeed, many teachers may feel that it is somehow wrong to approach literature in such an 'irreverent' way. This is understandable, because from our early schooldays we are encouraged to show reverence towards 'Literature', whatever our true feelings may be.

In fact, as we hope you will discover, there is nothing irreverent about the approaches in this book. Their aim is, simply, to use literary material to generate language. The students may or may not like a text, but at least they are free to say so. And they are not expected to admire the writing, any more than they are expected to admire a text on hydraulic pumps or on air pollution in a 'regular' language class.

About the activities

The first three activities all have a similar function, which is to raise the question: 'What is literature?' or 'What do we think it is?' The question, of course, is not asked directly, and no answer is expected. But the material is designed to bring to the surface certain assumptions about what is, or is not, literature.

So, for instance, in 1.1 *Opening lines*, the students are given the opening lines of ten different works – five poems and five pieces of non-fiction – and are asked to choose those they think might be drawn from poems. Could a poem begin: 'Water is H_2O, hydrogen two parts, oxygen one'? Unlikely perhaps, but possible.

Similar questions are followed up in 1.2 *Sources*, in which the material is drawn entirely from prose works, fiction and non-fiction. Both activities are suggesting the same concept, which is: literature is not a world apart. In many ways, it resembles 'ordinary' language. This concept recurs in 1.3 *Poetry or prose?* in which two of the four 'prose' passages are in fact poems written out in the form of prose.

We then move on to an activity based on dialogue, 1.4 *Split exchanges*. Here, we focus more closely on the text and on what is suggested by the words. The material is minimal, consisting of a remark, followed by a response to the remark. The two halves of the exchanges are presented separately, and the students are asked to suggest possible combinations. In this activity, they are learning to look closely at the text and to pick up whatever clues are there. For instance, a remark such as:

– 'You think she's a man-hater?'

could be followed by any of these responses:

– 'I do not – I *will* not believe that.'
– 'If you like.'
– '*She* thinks she is.'

The clue is contained in the repetition of *she* (in the third response). But the other suggestions would not be wrong. And this understanding, that in working with literature there may be several right responses, is vital to all further work.

The three activities that follow, 1.5 *Split poem*, 1.6 *Word portraits*, and 1.7 *Speculation 1*, all build on encouraging the suggestion of several possible responses. In two of the activities (*Split poem* and *Speculation*) the responses can be matched against the actual answer. In *Word portraits*, however, there are no conclusive answers. The students are free to defend their own interpretation of the text. Likewise, in activities 1.8 *Personal choice* and 1.9 *Odd man out*, the students are invited to offer plausible arguments rather than definitive answers.

The section concludes with a bridging activity, 1.10 *Authors' comments*, in which the students contrast their own reaction to dialogue with the comments provided by the author. This exercise in speculation will be explored more thoroughly in Section 2.

1.1 Opening lines

LEVEL
Elementary to intermediate

TIME
7 – 10 minutes

PREPARATION
Select the opening lines of five works of non-fiction and five poems. Prepare these to be shown on an overhead projector (OHP), or distributed to the students. (See sample texts.)

IN CLASS
1 The class works as one large group. Ask the students to decide which lines they think are the openings of poems. Do not at this stage tell them how many lines are drawn from poems.

2 After five minutes, ask the students to call out the lines which they think are not the openings of poems. Note the numbers on the board.

3 Now reveal that five of the lines are taken from poems. Ask the students to decide which these might be.

4 Then reveal the sources.

NOTES
1 Literature, particularly in a foreign language, is often seen as something remote and far removed from 'ordinary' language. One of the aims of this activity is to show that literature is not necessarily a language apart. Even poetry, if we do not know it is poetry, can be mistaken for plain prose. And plain prose may have its own poetry.

2 See also 1.3 *Poetry or prose?*

SOURCES
1 Kenneth Clark: *The Nude*
2 Nian Cheng: *Life and Death in Shanghai*
3 Nikolaus Pevsner: *An Outline of European Architecture*
4 D. H. Lawrence: *Collected Poems*
5 Ogden Nash: 'I want a drink of water, but not from the thermos'
6 Bertrand Russell: *The Problems of Philosophy*
7 Michael Swan: 'Nothing to Eat'
8 from an article in *The Independent*
9 D. J. Enright: 'The Municipal Waterbawd'
10 Philip Larkin: 'Sunny Prestatyn'

SAMPLE TEXTS
1 The English language, with its elaborate generosity, distinguishes between the naked and the nude.
2 The past is forever with me and I remember it all.
3 A bicycle shed is a building; Lincoln Cathedral is a piece of architecture.
4 Water is H_2O, hydrogen two parts, oxygen one; but there is also a third thing that makes it water.

5   Have you ever spent two and a half of your three hours allotted shopping time hunting for a place to park?

6   Is there any knowledge in the world which is so certain that no reasonable man could doubt it?

7   She had nothing to eat. They made a film about her because she had nothing to eat.

8   A young boy being led away from a station by his mother was brandishing a large knife with a serrated blade. It was plastic, but realistic.

9   The use of a hose for non-domestic purposes can be quite costly. And even more so if an automatic sprinkler is employed.

10 'Come to sunny Prestatyn', laughed the girl on the poster.

KEY

The opening lines of poems are numbers 4, 5, 7, 9, 10.

1.2 Sources

LEVEL

Intermediate

TIME

10 – 15 minutes

PREPARATION

1 Select five or six short passages from a variety of sources, at least two of which should be literary. (See sample texts for examples.)

2 Prepare enough copies for the whole class.

IN CLASS

1 Ask the students to read through the passages on their own and to mark those which they think are taken from literary sources, such as a play, novel, or short story.

2 After five minutes, the students form groups of four and compare their ideas. Ask them to underline in the texts any words or expressions which helped them to make their decisions.

3 Write up the sources, giving the author's name, the title, and a very brief description of the work, for instance, Des Carroll: 'Lifer' (autobiographical interview).

Ask the students to match each text with one of the titles.

4 *Round-up discussion.* Reveal the original matchings, and ask the students to call out any features of language which gave a clue to the source.

VARIATION

1 Give the students five texts and ten possible sources. This will lead to more discussion over which are the most likely matchings.

2 With more advanced students, one of the texts included could be a poem written out in the form of prose. (See also 1.3 *Poetry or prose?*)

NOTES

This activity encourages close attention to what is actually said in the text. In looking for clues, and in marking features of the language, the students are learning how to use the text itself in discussion. Focusing on the particular helps to discourage vague theorizing.

SOURCES

1 Thor Heyerdahl: *Aku-Aku*
2 Malcolm Bradbury: *The History Man*
3 Rijkshogeschool, Maastricht: 'Translating the Annual Company Report'.
4 Terry Kirby: an article in *The Independent*
5 Harold Pinter: *Silence*
6 Des Carroll: 'Lifer', an article in *SHE*

SAMPLE TEXTS

1 Not a soul was to be seen on shore, only a deserted, petrified world with motionless stone heads gazing at us from their distant ridge, while other equally motionless stone men lay prostrate in a row at the foot of a long terrace right in the foreground, on the lava blocks along the coast. It was as though we had anchored with a hovering spaceship off the shore of an extinct world, where once had lived beings of a kind other than those on our earth.

2 In 1970 the technotronic age became official; the Computing Centre was put into use, and it began work by issuing a card with a number on it to everyone on campus, telling them who they were, an increasingly valuable piece of information. And now the campus is massive, one of those dominant modern environments of multifunctionality that modern man creates.

3 Anyway, to finish off, I'll tell you what typically happens. It's always at about five to three on a Thursday afternoon; the Financial Director, who hasn't seen his wife for four weeks and can't remember what his children look like, wife is threatening to leave him, he decides that his work is finally done, and as I say, it's four minutes to three now, he's got his coat on, he's walking down the corridor, and he happens to pass an open door and he overhears a conversation . . .

4 Mid-evening in the grimy booking hall of Manor House underground station on the Piccadilly line in north London: the escalators rumble in the background as a vagrant shuffles aimlessly in and out. Scruffy youngsters hang around the newspaper kiosk. A middle-aged woman ticket inspector adopts a deliberately stern manner to deal with a smart young man who has tried to walk through without a ticket. After some discussion, he pays up.

5 After my work each day I walk back through people but I don't notice them. I'm not in a dream or anything of that sort. On the contrary. I'm quite wide awake to the world around me. But not to the people. There must be something in them to notice, to pay attention to, something of interest in them. In fact I know there is. I'm certain of it. But I pass through them noticing nothing.

6 We're locked away from eight at night till eight the next morning. After breakfast we're locked up, then again after lunch and after tea. It's about sixteen hours a day. Too bad if you're claustrophobic. There's no choice except madness or suicide. I've had attacks when I couldn't wait for the door to open. But I rarely think about being locked in a cell.

KEY

The passages from literary sources are numbers 2 and 5.

1.3 Poetry or prose?

LEVEL

Lower intermediate to advanced

TIME

10 – 15 minutes

PREPARATION

1 Select two or three short passages of prose which are in some way striking, because of their rhythm, use of language, imagery, and so on. Write these passages out in the form of poems. Then copy two or three short poems, without making any changes to the text. (For examples, see sample texts.)

2 Prepare sufficient copies of the passages for each group of four students to have one set.

IN CLASS

1 Divide the students into groups of four. Give each group a complete set of the passages you have chosen. Tell the students that certain of the passages were originally written in the form of prose. Ask them to mark those passages which they feel sure are poems, and those which they think must be prose texts.

2 After discussion, each group exchanges thoughts with another group.

VARIATION

1 Write out two or three poems in the form of prose, and select a number of real prose texts to complete the set.

2 Ask the students to work in pairs and to write out, in the form of poetry, any of the texts which they think are poems.

NOTES

1 Our reaction to language is partly shaped by the way in which the words are presented. Consider, for instance, passage 1 in the sample texts in this form:

Rats indeed take some getting used to.
There are said to be
as many rats as human beings
even in England
in the large towns,
but the life
they lead
is
subterranean.

This, in fact, is prose. But it could be read as a poem. It has some of the qualities of poetry: balance and rhythm, conciseness, and internal rhyme.

2 One of the aims of this activity is to suggest that there is no clear-cut dividing line between literature and everyday language. Literature is not a secret, fenced-off area to which the ordinary language student has no right of access.

SOURCES

1 Graham Greene: *A Sort of Life*
2 George Orwell: *Down and Out in Paris and London*
3 Alan Duff: a poem
4 Stevie Smith: a poem
5 Cyril Connolly: *The Unquiet Grave*
6 Michael Swan: a poem

SAMPLE TEXTS

1 **Rats**
Rats indeed take some getting used to.
There are said to be as many rats
as human beings, even in England
in the large towns,
but the life they lead
is subterranean.

Unless you go down into the sewers
or haunt the huge rubbish dumps
which lie beyond the waste buildings-lots
under a thin fume of smoke,
you are unlikely to meet a rat.

It needs an effort of imagination
in Piccadilly Circus to realize
that for every passing person
there is a rat
in the tunnels
underneath.

2 **Beggars**

Beggars do not work, it is said –
but then, what is *work*?

A navvy works by swinging a pick.
An accountant works by adding up figures.
A beggar works by standing out of doors
in all weathers.

It is a trade like any other;
quite useless, of course – but then,
many reputable trades are quite useless.
As a social type a beggar compares well
with scores of others.

He is honest – compared with the sellers
of most patent medicines;

high-minded – compared with
a Sunday newspaper proprietor;
amiable – compared with
a hire-purchase tout.
In short, a parasite –
but a fairly harmless parasite.

He seldom extracts more than a bare living
from the community – and he pays for it
over and over in suffering.

3 Wales

Dead
and no heavier than a bucket of water
the lamb hung from the farmer's hand
as he told us of the wind that had killed this one
and maybe another three, which he couldn't find.
'It happens every year,' he said,
swinging the lamb as he spoke.
'The cold catches them sudden and they die.'

Beside him the mother nuzzled
the white belly of her lamb.
'She'd nuzzle it alive if she could . . .'
His dog looked up as if to ask:
Now, can we go?

4 Mabel

Mabel was married last week
So now only Tom left

The doctor didn't like Arthur's cough

I have been in bed since Easter
A touch of the old trouble

I am downstairs today
As I write this
I can hear Arthur roaming overhead
He loves to roam
Thank heavens he has plenty of space to roam in

We have seven bedrooms
And an annexe . . .

Our char has left now
And a good riddance too
Wages are very high in Tonbridge

Write and tell me how you are, dear,
And the girls,
Phoebe and Rose
They must be a great comfort to you
Phoebe and Rose.

5 Everything and everybody eternally radiates
a dim light – for those who care to seek.

The strawberry hidden under the last leaf cries:
'Pick me'.
The forgotten book, in the forgotten bookshop,
screams to be discovered.
Dead authors cry: 'Read me'.
Dead friends say: 'Remember me'.
Dead ancestors whisper: 'Unearth me'.
Dead places: 'Revisit me'.
And sympathetic spirits, living and dead,
Are continually trying to enter into communion.

6 The girls in airports
are more beautiful than the girls in other places.
Poised and elegant
remote, cool, unattainable
they sit
and in the depths of their eyes
(if you can face the humiliating gaze
that returns your furtive leer)
you can read the knowledge
that they are rich and expensive
and in a few hours
will be in Cairo or Caracas or Chicago
while you are in Croydon
trying to change your Belgian francs
back into sterling.

1.4 Split exchanges

LEVEL	**All levels**
TIME	**10 – 15 minutes**
PREPARATION	1 Select twelve to fifteen short dialogue exchanges from short stories, novels, or plays.

Split each exchange into two parts: remark and response. Write out the remarks on one sheet (task sheet A), and the responses on another (task sheet B). For instance:

Task sheet A
'He's an astute man.'

Task sheet B
'He's bloody pompous.'

Number each remark and each response. The numbers should not be in matching order.

2 Prepare enough copies of each task sheet for one third of the class (each group of three students should have one between them).

IN CLASS

1 Ask the students to work in groups of three. Give each group a copy of task sheet A. Tell the students to read through the remarks, and to discuss the responses they would expect.

2 Then give each group task sheet B, and ask them to try to match each remark from A with a response from B. If they think several combinations are possible, these should be noted.

3 Let each group compare its decisions with another. Then reveal which remarks from A match the responses from B.

NOTES

1 This activity has several advantages:

a. the material is easy to find, and can be graded to suit the students' language level

b. exchanges can be selected in order to illustrate particular aspects of language, such as the use of the present continuous: 'What are you doing now?' (task sheet A), 'The guard is looking at us' (task sheet B)

c. the activity combines constraint with freedom: the material itself is controlled, but several combinations are possible.

2 You may need to remind the students that the aim is not to find the right answer, but to look for plausible combinations. They should also be encouraged to speculate about the context in which the exchanges occur.

3 Much of the material can be drawn from passages which will be worked on more extensively in other activities. This, then, is a useful warm-up exercise. (For further ideas, see Maley and Duff: *Drama Techniques in Language Learning.*)

TASK SHEET A

The remarks below are all taken from dialogue exchanges in works of fiction. Match each remark with one of the responses given in task sheet B. If you feel that several responses are possible, note your alternative choices.

1 'Can't you bring yourself ever to forgive me?'
2 'Look, I'll tell you what I know from the beginning, only it will take some time, I am afraid . . .'
3 'What do you think of her? Is she not very charming?'
4 'Never marry! This is a new resolution!'
5 And do you think it takes one long to get used to this country?'
6 'You think she's a man-hater?'
7 'He's an astute man.'
8 'I would like to know.'
9 'Tell me what goes on. What are you doing now?'
10 'And you find life happier now?'
11 'Do you want me to kiss you in a way that is not tired?'
12 'It is beyond my powers – the powers of far wiser men than myself – to help you here.'

TASK SHEET B	Below are the responses made to the remarks given in task sheet A. Match each response with one or several of the remarks.

1 'If you like.'
2 '*She* thinks she is.'
3 'He's bloody pompous.'
4 'Never, never! I wouldn't marry you if you were the last man on earth.'
5 'I do not – I *will* not believe that.'
6 The guard is looking at us. I am putting the fishing-rod together.'
7 'Oh! yes – very – a very pleasing young woman.'
8 'Infinitely.'
9 'It would be better if you didn't know.'
10 'You mean you know why Mrs Turner was murdered?'
11 'Well, I should say it takes about four or five years for your blood properly to thin down.'
12 'It is one that I shall never change, however.'

KEY TO TASKS	A1/B4 – George Orwell: *Burmese Days*
	A2/B10 – Doris Lessing: *The Grass is Singing*
	A3/B7 – Jane Austen: *Emma*
	A4/B12 – Jane Austen: *Emma*
	A5/B11 – D. H. Lawrence: *Kangaroo*
	A6/B2 – D. H. Lawrence: *Sons and Lovers*
	A7/B3 – Brian Friel: *Translations*
	A8/B9 – H. E. Bates: *Fair Stood the Wind for France*
	A9/B6 – H. E. Bates: *Fair Stood the Wind for France*
	A10/B8 – D. H. Lawrence: *Sons and Lovers*
	A11/B1 – H. E. Bates: *Fair Stood the Wind for France*
	A12/B5 – John Fowles: *The French Lieutenant's Woman*

VARIATION	**Speaking the exchanges**

PREPARATION	Instead of giving the groups the two task sheets to read, cut each sheet into twelve separate slips. If you have more than twenty-four students in the class, prepare more exchanges.

IN CLASS	Ask the students to walk around the room and speak to everyone in the class. They should say only what is written on their slip of paper. Each student tries to find at least one partner with a matching slip.

SOURCES	1 Willy Russell: *Educating Rita*
	2 Paul Theroux: *The London Embassy*
	3 D. H. Lawrence: *Kangaroo*
	4 Anton Chekov: *Short Stories*
	5 Somerset Maugham: *The Moon and Sixpence*
	6 Joseph Conrad: *The Secret Sharer*

EXAMPLES

1   - I want to talk to you about this that you sent me.
    - That? Oh ...

2   - Shall we do this again some time?
    - Again and again. Would you like that?

3   - You don't think much of Australia, then?
    - Why, how am I to judge?

4   - Now, what *is* the matter?
    - Oh, it's nothing, nothing. Go away. Can't you see I'm not dressed?

5   - Has anything happened?
    - My wife has left me.

6   - I say, no need to call anyone.
    - I was not going to.

7   - Someone will go for her with a bread knife one day - and he won't miss her!
    - I'm not so sure.

8   - I'm sorry I was late. It was unavoidable.
    - What's wrong with your voice? Why can't you talk properly?

9   - Speaking out may get you into trouble.
    - It's often done so in the past.

10 - I don't want you to make fun of me.
    - Don't you?

11 - Twenty-five minutes past five.
    - I had imagined it was later.

12 - I wanted to ask you something.
    - Did you? What was it?

13 - You should take off your shoes before entering the mosque.
    - I already have.

14 - Tell me, what kind of man do you prefer?
    - Oh, I've never thought of it.

15 - Why are you going to marry him?
    - He's got pots of money. I'm nearly twenty-six.

1.5 Split poem

LEVEL	**Intermediate to advanced**
TIME	**20 minutes**

PREPARATION

1 For this activity you will need a short poem (twelve to sixteen lines) which has a fairly regular form. That is, the lines should be of roughly equal length.

2 Split each line into two parts, and place the half lines under separate columns (A and B). The first half of each line goes under column A, the second under column B. For instance:

They are going home/to working wives
To cooling beds/at breakfast time

A	B
They are going home	to working wives
To cooling beds	at breakfast time

Then arrange the half lines in each column so that they are not in matching order. (See task sheet. The full version of the text follows the task sheet.)

3 Prepare enough copies of the split poem for one third of the class.

IN CLASS

1 Read the poem aloud to the whole class (or play a recording of the text). Ask the students to recall any fragments they can remember.

2 (Optional) Let the students hear the poem once again, but do not ask them to recall the text.

3 Ask the students to work in groups of three. Give each group a copy of the split poem. Ask them to try to reconstruct the poem by matching the half lines from columns A and B.

4 *Round-up session.* The class, working as a single group, builds up the poem line by line.

VARIATION

With advanced students, the activity can be made more challenging by leaving out the reading of the poem (*In class*, steps 1 and 2), and by asking the groups to work immediately from the split text. They should look for several different possible combinations of the half lines, and then gradually try to construct the poem.

NOTES

1 This activity was originally devised to be presented in the way described under *Variation*. However, experience at seminars has shown that teachers generally find this approach too difficult. The modified approach, which begins with listening to the poem, has proved far more popular and by no means too easy.

2 This step-by-step approach allows the students to work their way gradually from the language towards the meaning. It is particularly suitable for poems which contain striking or unusual images, for example: 'They live in a dislocation of hours/Inside-out like socks pulled on in darkness.'

3 After working with the poem in this way, the students will be familiar with the text. The poem can then appear again, as an 'old friend', in other activities, such as 3.4 *Discussion topics 1*.

TASK SHEET

With your partners, try to reconstruct the poem by matching the half lines from column A with those of column B.

Night-Shift Workers

A	B
And ears grew numb	in a dislocation of hours
Going out to work	unlike others
They live	in the sky together
They have come	from their skin like clothes
Soft as fur	from a factory
Where sun and moon shine	to working wives
Where fluorescent strips	at breakfast time
To cooling beds	flared all night
Undressing fatigue	in darkness
Waking	to machinery
They are going home	and taste teeth
Later to wake at four	in the morning
Inside-out like socks pulled on	when the day is over
They are always at an ebb	in their mouths

SAMPLE TEXT

Night-Shift Workers

They have come from a factory
Where fluorescent strips flared all night
And ears grew numb to machinery.
They are going home to working wives,
To cooling beds at breakfast time,
Undressing fatigue from their skin like clothes.
Later to wake at four and taste teeth
Soft as fur in their mouths.
They live in a dislocation of hours
Inside-out like socks pulled on in darkness
Waking when the day is over.
They are always at an ebb, unlike others
Going out to work in the morning
Where sun and moon shine in the sky together.

(George Charlton: 'New Angles')

1.6 Word portraits

LEVEL

Intermediate to advanced

TIME

15 minutes

PREPARATION

1 From a novel, short story, or autobiography, select a striking character sketch. (Two examples are given in the sample texts.)

2 Make enough copies for the whole class.

3 Prepare for each character a short list of prompts. These should be words or expressions which might or might not apply to the character described. In making the lists, try *not* to use words which actually appear in the text.

Here are two specimen lists, one for each of the texts.

Text 1

shy	soft-spoken
dirty	smartly dressed
clumsy	proud
pedantic	punctual
sarcastic	self-centred
talkative	impatient
modest	strict

Text 2

skinny	vain
sharp-tongued	elegant
generous	eager to please
sociable	kind
strong-willed	possessive
hypocritical	highly intelligent

IN CLASS

1 Give each student a copy of one of the texts you have chosen, and allow four to five minutes for silent reading.

2 While the students are reading, write up the prompt words (see *Preparation*) on the board or on an OHP transparency.

3 Ask the students to form groups of three, and to decide which of the prompt words are most and which are least appropriate to the character. For each prompt word, they should find words or lines in the text to support their decision.

4 *Class discussion.* Run through the list of prompt words, and ask the class to give their views. (An economical way of recording their reactions is to mark each prompt word on the board with a tick (√), a minus sign (−), or a question mark (?) to indicate whether the word is wholly appropriate, not appropriate, or only partly appropriate.)

NOTES

1 A composition question often seen in textbooks is: 'Describe in your own words the character of . . .' This often results in stilted, uninteresting answers: the students are frustrated because they feel

they have nothing to add to what the author has already said. And any attempt to 'describe the character in your own words' is likely to be superficial because characters are complex and cannot always be pinned down by a few neat adjectives.

In this activity, we have inverted the traditional approach. Instead of working out from the text towards rough generalizations, the students work back to the text from a general prompt. And instead of reducing the character, they expand it by discovering how much is implied but not stated in the text.

2 An illustration may help to clarify what we have just said. A group of students in Austria, working on sample text A, unanimously agreed that the guitar teacher was 'soft-spoken'. But they could find no evidence in the text. Then one student said: 'Well, the writer says "he knocked softly at my door and entered on tiptoe . . .". I can't imagine a man with a loud voice doing that.'

This was an important remark, because it shows that the impressions we gain from a literary text are often implied rather than stated.

In India, a group reacted in a similar way to a passage from Jane Austen's *Northanger Abbey*. In this case, the text was longer (a full chapter) involving mainly dialogue between two young women, Catherine and Isabella. Twelve prompt words were given, which might have applied to either character. One of these words was *elegant*. All agreed that Isabella was and Catherine was not 'elegant'. Jane Austen did not say so, but she did imply it through the dialogue.

3 *Language*. There are two ways in which you can monitor the language level:
a. through your choice of text (text A, we suggest, is less demanding than text B)
b. through your choice of prompt words, for example, *proud* instead of *conceited*.

4 *Pictures*. A set of photographs or portraits of people can be used to complement the prompt words. Show the students the photographs and ask them which picture comes closest to their impression of the character. (See p. 71.)

SAMPLE TEXT A   But to be in Seville without a guitar is like being on ice without skates. So every morning, while Kati went dancing with the Maestro Realito, I took lessons on the instrument in my room.

My instructor, one of Seville's most respected professors of the guitar, was a small sad man, exquisitely polite and patient, poorly but neatly dressed, and addicted to bow-ties made of wallpaper. Each day, at the stroke of ten, he knocked softly at my door and entered on tiptoe, as though into a sick room, carrying his guitar-case like a doctor's bag.

'How are we today?' he would ask sympathetically, 'and how do we proceed?'

Silently, he would place two chairs opposite each other, put me in the one facing the light, sit himself in the other, and then ponder me long and sadly while I played. Infinite compassion, as from one who has seen much suffering, possessed his face while he listened. An expression also of one who, forced to inhabit a solitary peak of perfection, has nowhere to look but downwards at the waste of a fumbling world.

After an hour's examination, during which he tested all my faulty coordinations, he would hand me a page of exercises and bid me take them twice a day. Then, with a little bow, his chin resting mournfuly upon his paper tie, he would leave me to visit his next patient.

Sometimes – but only very occasionally – he would relax at the end of the lesson, empty his pockets of tobacco dust, roll himself a cigarette, smile, and take up his guitar and play to me for an hour. Then his eyes would turn inward and disappear into the echoing chambers of his mind, while his long white fingers moved over the strings with the soft delicacy of the blind, lost in a dream of melody and invention. And faced with the beauty of his technique, the complex harmonies, the ease and grace, the supreme mastery of tone and feeling, I would feel like one of the lesser apes who, shuffling on his knuckles through the sombre marshes, suddenly catches sight of homo sapiens, upright on a hill, his gold head raised to the sky.

(Laurie Lee: *Cider with Rosie*)

SAMPLE TEXT B

The Lovely Lady

At seventy-two, Pauline Attenborough could still sometimes be mistaken, in the half-light, for thirty. She really was a wonderfully preserved woman, of perfect *chic*. Of course, it helps a great deal to have the right frame. She would be an exquisite skeleton, and her skull would be an exquisite skull, like that of some Etruscan woman, with feminine charm still in the swerve of the bone and the pretty naïve teeth.

Mrs Attenborough's face was of the perfect oval, and slightly flat type that wears best. There is no flesh to sag. Her nose rode serenely, in its finely bridged curve. Only her big grey eyes were a tiny bit prominent on the surface of her face, and they gave her away most. The bluish lids were heavy, as if they ached sometimes with the strain of keeping the eyes beneath them arch and bright; and at the corners of the eyes were fine little wrinkles which would slacken with haggardness, then be pulled up tense again, to that bright, gay look like a Leonardo woman who really could laugh outright.

Her niece Cecilia was perhaps the only person in the world who was aware of the invisible little wire which connected Pauline's eye-wrinkles with Pauline's will-power. Only Cecilia *consciously* watched the eyes go haggard and old and tired, and remain so, for hours; until Robert came home. Then ping!—the mysterious little wire that worked between Pauline's will and her face went taut, the wary, haggard, prominent eyes suddenly began to gleam, the eyelids arched, the queer curved eyebrows which floated in such frail arches on Pauline's forehead began to gather a mocking significance, and you had the *real* lovely lady, in all her charm.

She really had the secret of everlasting youth; that is to say, she could don her youth again like an eagle. But she was sparing of it. She was wise enough not to try being young for too many people. Her son Robert, in the evenings, and Sir Wilfred Knipe sometimes in the afternoon to tea; then occasional visitors on Sunday, when Robert was home; for these she was her lovely and changeless self, that age could not wither, nor custom stale; so bright and kindly and yet subtly mocking, like Mona Lisa who knew a thing or two. But Pauline knew more, so she needn't be smug at all, she could laugh that lovely mocking Bacchante laugh of hers, which was at the same time never malicious, always good-naturedly tolerant, both of virtues and vices. The former, of course, taking much more tolerating. So she suggested, roguishly.

Only with her niece Cecilia she did not trouble to keep up the glamour. Ciss was not very observant, anyhow; and more than that, she was plain; more still, she was in love with Robert; and most of all, she was thirty, and dependent on her Aunt Pauline. Oh, Cecilia! Why make music for her!

(D. H. Lawrence: *The Lovely Lady*)

1.7 Speculation 1

LEVEL	**All levels**
TIME	**15 – 20 minutes**
PREPARATION	**1** Select three or four short texts containing mostly dialogue and very little description. Particularly suitable for this activity are dialogue exchanges which are tense and terse, for instance:

'What do we do?'
'We drive straight in.'

or:

'I say, no need to call anyone.'
'I was not going to.'

2 For each passage, write out three brief explanations, one of which is the real interpretation.

3 Prepare copies of the text of your choice and the task sheet for one third of the class.

IN CLASS

1 Divide the class into groups of three. Give each group a copy of the passages. Ask the students to think of any possible explanations of what is happening:
– *Who are the speakers?*
– *Where are they?*
– *Why are they together?*
– *What is happening, or going to happen?*

2 After discussion, the groups exchange ideas.

3 Now give each group a copy of the possible explanations. Tell them that there are three explanations for each passage, but they are not given in order. Two are invented, one is real. Ask them to choose the one they prefer in each case.

4 Allow time for discussion before you reveal which explanations are the real ones.

NOTES

1 It is important to remind the students that the purpose of the activity is not to guess the right explanation, but to speculate on what the words might mean, that is, the students create their own context. However, it is natural for students to want to know the answer. This is why answers are given at the end of the activity.

2 In *In class* steps 1 and 2, you may find that the discussion is very uneven. Some students may have many ideas, others none at all. If any groups become stuck, let them see the explanation sheet at an earlier stage. This will help to focus their discussion.

3 *Language.* One of the virtues of this activity is that it can be based on linguistically simple material. It is not hard to find dialogue exchanges which even near-beginners can understand. And the explanations do not need to be complex. Yet advanced students can also enjoy working on this 'simple' material because, unlike many of the dialogues in textbooks, it is not self-explanatory, and is open to interpretation.

4 For further material illustrating a similar approach, see Maley and Duff: *Variations on a Theme.*

SOURCES AND KEY

1 Gustave Flaubert: *Madame Bovary* (explanation 8)
2 H. E. Bates: *Fair Stood the Wind for France* (explanation 9)
3 Joseph Conrad: *The Secret Sharer* (explanation 7)

SAMPLE TEXTS

1 He rose to go; and as if the movement had been the signal for their flight, Emma said, suddenly assuming a gay air:
'You have the passports?'
'Yes.'
'You are forgetting nothing?'
'No.'
'Are you sure?'
'Certainly.'
'It is at the Hôtel de Provence, is it not, that you will wait for me at midday?'
He nodded.
'Till tomorrow, then!' said Emma in a last caress; and she watched him go. He did not turn round.

2 'What is the procedure in this town?' he said. 'Shall we be stopped?'

'There is no procedure,' the girl said. 'Some days they stop you, and some days they don't stop you. That's all.'

'What do we do?'

'We drive straight in.'

'It seems very obvious.'

'It is better to do the obvious thing. Better than trying to be clever.'

3 'What's the matter?' I asked in my ordinary tone, speaking down to the face upturned exactly under mine.

'Cramp,' it answered, no louder. Then slightly anxious, 'I say, no need to call any one.'

'I was not going to,' I said.

'Are you alone on deck?'

'Yes.'

'I suppose your captain's turned in?'

TASK SHEET

Below are some brief explanations of the passages you have just read. Some are invented, others are true. For each passage, select one explanation only.

1 The year is 1956. Two refugees from Eastern Europe are talking together in a hotel room in Brussels. They suspect that someone is listening at the door. She talks loudly and clearly, to make sure that whoever is listening hears the *wrong* information.

2 A wealthy, ageing film producer describes in his autobiography how he moored his private yacht in a small Mediterranean port. He is tired of being pursued by journalists in Nice, Monaco, Cannes. One evening, while looking out to sea, he notices a swimmer clinging to his rope ladder. Another journalist? Probably. But she is most attractive. He pretends, for the moment, to be a member of the crew.

3 The scene takes place in Spain, at the height of the Inquisition. Emma (Emilia) is the daughter of a rich banker from Valladolid. Her father, knowing that he would be imprisoned by the Inquisition, arranged for his daughter to flee to France with a trustworthy young man. But can the young man be trusted?

4 The scene takes place in provincial France at the height of the revolutionary terror. An Englishman, the 'Scarlet Pimpernel', who helps French noblemen to escape to England, is now himself in great danger. He is being pursued. A young peasant girl, however, agrees to help him. Disguised in worker's clothes, he will drive with her in the farm cart, through the town and to safety.

5 The scene takes place in a small bay along the coast of Florida. An American coastguard, disguised as an ordinary yachtsman, is waiting to trap a small boat run by drug smugglers. While he is waiting, a swimmer suddenly appears alongside. The coastguard suspects he may be one of the smugglers.

6 A remote town in South America has been taken over by a fanatical religious sect. One of the members, a girl of seventeen has secretly written to a journalist asking him to write an exposé of the sect. The first and most dangerous step is to introduce him unnoticed into the town.

7 The time is around 1880. The captain of an old-fashioned sailing ship is becalmed in the south China sea, miles from land (the nearest land is the bottom of the sea!). It is night. As he looks over the side of the boat, he sees a man in the water. The captain is astonished. Where could the man have come from? But he remains outwardly calm.

8 An attractive woman in her mid-30s, unhappily married to a man of provincial importance (in 19th century France), is planning to elope the next day with her young, wealthy lover. He, in fact, will not come to the rendezvous.

9 It is wartime in occupied France (1943). An injured British pilot, who has been sheltered by a sympathetic farmer, is being well cared for by the farmer's daughter. However, to obtain supplies, they must go to the nearest (occupied) town. She does not dare to go alone, and her father cannot go with her. The pilot must go with her.

1.8 Personal choice

LEVEL

Lower intermediate to advanced

TIME

20 minutes

PREPARATION

1 Select four short poems (ten to twenty lines) which you think your students will understand without much difficulty, and make copies, one for each student.

2 Then prepare a questionnaire on the following lines:

Questionnaire

Read through the four poems you are given. Then decide which poem and which lines you would choose in response to the questions.

1 If you had to *translate* one of the poems, which would it be?
  Which line(s) would you find most difficult?

2 If you were asked to *illustrate* one of the poems with a photograph or a sketch, which would you choose?
  Which line(s) would provide the focus for your illustrations?

3 If somebody wanted to *set one of the poems to music*, which would you suggest?
  Are there any lines which could be repeated, as a refrain?

4 If you had the chance of talking to all four poets, *which would you most like to meet*?
  Which line(s) would you ask him or her to explain?

---

3 Make enough copies of the questionnaire for one third of the class.

IN CLASS

1 Give each student a copy of the poems. Allow four to five minutes for silent reading.

2 (Optional) Ask the students to turn over the sheet so that they cannot see the texts, and to note down any words or lines they can remember.

3 Ask the students to form groups of three, and give each group a copy of the questionnaire. (See *Preparation*.)

After ten minutes, each group joins another to compare their responses.

NOTES

1 You will notice that the one question which is not directly asked in the questionnaire is: Which poem do you like best/least? The reason for not asking this is that the question rarely yields a satisfactory answer. It is very difficult, particularly in a foreign language, to say why you do or do not like a piece of writing. However, in responding to question 1 (Which poem would you choose to translate?), the students are free to discuss the question of personal likes and dislikes if they want to.

2 Another question which is deliberately not raised is that of quality. The students are not required to say whether they think a poem is good or bad. But they are given an opportunity to comment on quality in a direct, down-to-earth way by selecting certain lines for special attention.

3 This activity illustrates what we meant in the main *Introduction* by using literature for language practice, just as we would use any other material.

SOURCES

1 Roger McGough: 'Storm'
2 Verity Bargate: 'Wasp Poem'
3 Michael Swan: 'Nothing to Eat'
4 W. B. Yeats: 'He Wishes for the Cloths of Heaven'

SAMPLE TEXTS

1 Storm

They're at it again
the wind and the rain
It all started
when the wind
took the window
by the collar
and shook it
with all its might
Then the rain
butted in
What a din
they'll be at it all night
Serves them right
if they go home in the morning
and the sky won't let them in.

2 Wasp Poem

Today I drowned a wasp that I
Found floating in my wine.
Its life no longer is its own,
but neither is it mine.
With cool precision turned by hate
I drowned it in the sink –
it struggled in the water
but I didn't stop to think.
I didn't feel a pang at all,
I didn't change my mind,
I didn't even, really, feel
that this was cruel, unkind.
If metamorphosis exists
perhaps a wasp I'll be
and I won't feel resentment
if you do the same to me.
I may regret the sunshine,
the pollen and the jam,
but I'll understand you're drowning me
because I'm what I am.

3 Nothing to Eat

She had nothing to eat.
They made a film about her
because she had nothing to eat.

Her husband
was killed in the war.
They wrote a book about
how he was killed in the war.

Her brother and mother
were executed by the revolutionary guards.
There was an opera about it.

Both her children died
(there was no hospital).
You can see the photographs
at an exhibition in London.

Then somebody wrote a poem.

Still
she had nothing to eat.

4 He Wishes for the Cloths of Heaven

Had I the heavens' embroidered cloths,
Enwrought with golden and silver light,
The blue and the dim and the dark cloths
Of night and light and the half-light,
I would spread the cloths under your feet:
But I, being poor, have only my dreams;
I have spread my dreams under your feet;
Tread softly because you tread on my dreams.

1.9 Odd man out

LEVEL

Intermediate

TIME

15 – 20 minutes

PREPARATION

For each student, make sets of three short texts which are in some way similar. For example, they deal with the same theme, they are comparable in register (formal or informal), or they are drawn from similar sources.

One of the passages should have a particular feature which makes it stand out from the other two (one text might be a satire or parody, or one might be different in meaning from the others).

IN CLASS

Give the students the task sheets, and ask them to decide which is the odd man out, and why.

NOTES

1 The main drawback of this activity is that it takes some time to prepare. However, it also has several advantages:

a. It is a useful warm-up activity. Students enjoy trying to spot the odd man out. (You may need to remind them that there is no final answer: the odd man out could be any of the passages, provided the students can give reasons to justify their answers.)

b. The activity requires close attention to the use of language. It also trains students to refer back to the text in their reasoning.

c. It gives you the opportunity to introduce texts which the students may work on later in greater depth in other activities.

SOURCES

1 a) Fred Hoyle: *The Nature of the Universe*
   b) Jane Austen: *Northanger Abbey*
   c) John Osborne: *Look Back in Anger*

2 a) *Mostar: a guide*
   b) Eric Newby: *The Big Red Train Ride*
   c) *Edinburgh: A guide to the city*

3 a) Edmund Spenser: a sonnet
   b) Roger McGough: 'Valerie'
   c) Edmund Waller: 'Go Lovely Rose!'

TASK SHEET

In each of the sets of passages below, one text stands out as being in some way different from the other two. Decide which is the 'odd man out' and why.

1 a) You might like to ask why the Sun is able to supply its own light, heat, and energy, whereas the Earth and the other planets only shine feebly with the aid of borrowed light. Strange as it may seem, it is best to start this problem by considering the interior of the Earth.

  b) The morrow brought a very sober-looking morning, the sun making only a few efforts to appear; and Catherine augured from it everything most favourable to her wishes. A bright morning so early in the year, she allowed, would generally turn to rain; but a cloudy one foretold improvement as the day advanced.

  c) Your mother and I were so happy then. It seemed as though we had everything we could ever want. I think the last day the sun shone was when that dirty little train steamed out of that crowded, suffocating Indian station, and the battalion band playing for all it was worth. I knew in my heart it was all over then. Everything.

2 a) Just as Paris would not be what it is without the Seine, or Leningrad without the Neva, or Vienna without the Danube, so Mostar would not be what it is if there were no Neretva. Reaching the town from the north, the river divides it with its green waters and unites it with its bridges.

  b) Leningrad is a city of canals, a northern Venice of such beauty that there is no absurdity in the comparison, and as the taxi raced down the Nevski Prospekt, over what looked like pure ice, it seemed, with the huge flakes of snow drifting down into it out of the darkness of the northern night, yet another enchanted, frozen waterway.

  c) Edinburgh is a city unlike any other. It has been called 'the Athens of the North' and had its site compared with the sevens hills on which Rome was built. But Athens ('the Edinburgh of the South'?) is in truth not more dramatic to look at, and if you search diligently you can find at least a dozen hills within the Edinburgh boundaries.

3 a) My love is like to ice, and I to fire:
     How comes it then that this her cold so great
     Is not dissolved through my so hot desire?

  b) Discretion is the better part of Valerie
     (though all of her is nice)
     lips as warm as strawberries
     eyes as cold as ice.

c) Go, lovely Rose!
Tell her, that wastes her time and me,
That now she knows,
When I resemble her to thee,
How sweet and fair she seems to be.

KEY TO TASKS

The odd man out in each set could be:

1 a) because it is not from a literary source
   c) because *the sun* is used metaphorically here: 'the last day the
      sun shone' = the last day I was truly happy. (In passages **a**
      and **b**, the sun is simply the sun.)

2 b) because it is not taken from a tourist brochure
   a) because there is no direct comparison between one city and
      another, as there is in **b** (Leningrad . . . a northern Venice),
      and **c** (Edinburgh . . . 'the Athens of the North').

3 c) because the poet is praising, not criticizing, his love
   b) because the language is 'modern' (passages **a** and **c** are both
      from the 17th century).

1.10 Authors' comments

LEVEL

Intermediate

TIME

15 – 20 minutes

PREPARATION

1 From novels or short stories, select a number of short passages of
dialogue which also include comments by the author on how the
characters speak. For instance:

'Has anything happened?' I asked.
'My wife has left me.'
He could hardly get the words out.

2 Remove some of the authors' comments from the passages (in
this case, *He could hardly get the words out*), and list these comments
on a separate sheet. Then write out the passages leaving gaps for the
missing comments. Number each of the gaps. (See sample texts.)

3 Make enough copies of the sample texts and authors' comments
for one third of the class.

IN CLASS

1 Ask the students to work in groups of three. Give each group a
copy of the sample texts. Explain that the gaps in the text indicate
places where a comment by the author has been left out. Ask the
students to suggest how they think the words were spoken in each
case (hesitantly? roughly? softly?).

2 Each group exchanges suggestions with another.

3 Now hand out copies of the authors' comments, not in matching order. Ask the students to choose an appropriate comment for each gap. If several comments seem suitable, they should note their preferences.

4 After a short round-up discussion, reveal the original combinations.

NOTES

1 The passages used in this activity should be sufficiently long to give the students a clear picture of the speakers and of their relationship to one another. When you first try out the activity, you could make it easier by using only one, or perhaps two, of the sample texts.

2 The activity is, in fact, a form of reading comprehension. In trying to guess what kind of comments the author might have made (*In class*, steps 1 and 2), the students are searching for clues in the text. In text 3, for instance, we are told that Meg had taken 'the most instant dislike' to the strange man who climbed into her car. Therefore, when he says his first words ('How kind') there must be something in his voice that irritates Meg.

This is the kind of conclusion the students should be reaching in their discussion. Later, when they are asked to select the most suitable comment from the list, they will be looking for a remark which matches their own suggestions, even though it may be differently worded (He said *in a reedy, pedagogic voice*).

3 See also the *Notes* to the companion activity (2.7 *Suggesting the words*).

KEY

Original wording:

1	c	6	o	11	d
2	h	7	l	12	e
3	m	8	a	13	f
4	j	9	g	14	n
5	i	10	k	15	b

SAMPLE TEXTS

1 'Can I come in?' he asked.

In the dimness of the landing I could not see him very well, but there was something in his voice (1) . . . I led the way into my sitting-room and asked him to sit down.

'Thank God I've found you,' he said.

'What's the matter?' I asked (2) . . .

I was able now to see him well. As a rule he was neat in his person, but now his clothes were in disorder. I was convinced he had been drinking, and I smiled.

'I didn't know where to go,' he (3) . . . 'I came here earlier, but you weren't in.'

I changed my mind: it was not liquor that had driven him to this obvious desperation. His hands trembled.

'Has anything happened?' I asked.

'My wife has left me.'

He (4) . . .

(Somerset Maugham: *The Moon and Sixpence*)

2 I rang him up, without stopping to think how late it was: he was in, and I asked him to come round. In half an hour he came. We settled down on the hearthrug, holding hands and drinking Maxwell House. I don't know in what direction we were heading because just as I was settling down into a warm, companionable and harmless embrace the 'phone rang.

'Damn, damn, damn,' I said. 'Who the hell can that be at this time of night?'

'Don't answer it,' he said. This I took to be (5) . . ., so I didn't answer it. But it went on and on ringing, until on the twenty-sixth ring I felt I had to reply. I thought it might be an accident.

I lifted up the receiver and said my number (6) . . .

'Sarah, is that you?' It was Louise.

'Louise,' I said (7) . . ., and speaking straight to her for the first time in my life. 'Louise, what in God's name do you mean by ringing people up at this unspeakable hour of night. I've never heard of anything so absurd.'

'Look, Sarah, I'm terribly sorry to have woken you,' she said (8) . . ., on the other end of the line. 'I couldn't think what to do. The most awful unspeakable thing has happened. I simply can't believe it . . .' She sounded (9) . . ., and her voice (10) . . .

'You mean you're going to have a baby?' I said (11) . . ., as this was the sort of event that usually calls forth such incredulous clamour.

'Oh no,' she said (12) . . . 'Nothing as corny as that, but just as stupid.'

(Margaret Drabble: *A Summer Bird-Cage*)

3 (Meg has stopped on the motorway at night to pick up a girl who is hitch-hiking . . .) 'Please get in,' Meg said, and leaned over to open the door beside her. Then two things happened at once. The girl simply got into the back of the car – Meg heard her open the door and shut it gently, and a man, wearing a large black overcoat and a soft black hat tilted over his forehead slid into the seat beside her.

'How kind,' he said (13) . . . (almost as though he was practising to be someone else, Meg thought); 'we were wondering whether anyone at all would come to our aid, and it proves that charming young women like yourself behave as they appear. The Good Samaritan is invariably feminine these days.'

Meg, who had taken the most instant dislike to him of anyone she had ever met in life, said (14) . . . Then, beginning to feel bad about this, she asked:

'How far are you going?'

'Ah, now that will surprise you. My secretary and I broke down this morning on our way up, or down to Town,' he (15) . . .; 'and it is imperative that we present ourselves in the right place at the right time this evening.'

(Elizabeth Jane Howard: *Mr Wrong*)

Authors' comments:

a agitated
b sniggered
c that surprised me
d snappily
e brightly, catching my tone of voice
f in a reedy, pedagogic voice
g tremulous
h in astonishment at his vehemence
i an indication of affection
j could hardly get the words out
k faded away
l furiously
m burst out
n nothing at all
o crossly

2 General approaches

Introduction

Have you ever said to yourself: 'I've got good material, but I'm not sure how to use it'? If you have, you will be in good company. Many teachers make this remark.

This is why we have devoted one entire section (and an Appendix) to approaches which can be used with many different kinds of material. We should add, however, that these general approaches are not blanket approaches. They cannot be used indiscriminately on just any text. For each approach, certain materials will be more suitable than others.

In Section 1, we already suggested certain activities which could be extended and expanded by using different materials. Three examples are 1.6 *Word portraits*, 1.7 *Speculation 1*, and 1.8 *Personal choice*. Here, in Section 2, we show how these and other approaches can be developed.

Before we move on to the activities themselves, there are two general points which should be raised:

1 *Flexibility*. Any text can be approached in several different ways, depending on what aspect you choose to focus on: language, theme, depiction of character, or physical detail. It is possible, therefore, to use a text first in one way and then to come back to it using a different approach. For example, students can work on fragments of dialogue (as in 1.4 *Split exchanges*) without needing to know the context. Later, they can consider these same fragments in a fuller context (as in 2.7 *Suggesting the words*, or in 4.4 *Translation 1*).

2 *Similarity*. All texts, of course, are different. But they will have features in common. Descriptions of places and people tend to follow a similar pattern (see 2.6 *Character sketches*), and dialogue may be presented with or without the author's comment (see 1.10 *Authors' comments* and 2.7 *Suggesting the words*). The function of a general approach is to point out these similarities in texts, and so make it easier for you to find further material to suit the activity.

About the activities

As we mentioned in the main *Introduction*, one of the great advantages of literature is its suggestive power. What is meant is usually more than what is said. For instance, in 2.7 *Suggesting the words*, text 2:

Mama Who is this friend of yours?
Me   A girl called Gill Slater.
Mama And what does she do?
Me   Oh, she's a – she's a sort of research student.
Mama Oh yes? Well, it sounds like a very nice idea.

When 'Mama' says 'it sounds like a very nice idea', this is clearly *not* what she means. 'Mama' is worried about the idea of her daughter sharing a flat with a friend in London, far away from home.

In the activities, we have tried to show how this suggestive power in literature can be drawn out. Hence the emphasis on *speculation* – predicting what might happen, or what might be said – in activities such as *2.2 Speculation 2*, *2.3 Storylines 1*, *2.6 Character sketches*, *2.7 Suggesting the words*.

Many other activities in this book are also suitable for speculation, including *3.2 Creating situations from dialogue*, and *4.11 Writing*.

In *General approaches*, we have also suggested ways of dealing with longer texts, such as novels and short stories (see *2.3 Storylines 1* and *2.8 Completing the picture*), without requiring the students to read the full text in advance. And, for teachers with a taste for classical literature, we have included a short activity (*2.1 Quote unquote*) which may help to give fresh life to over-familiar set works or examination texts.

2.1 Quote unquote

LEVEL

Intermediate

TIME

15 – 20 minutes

PREPARATION

1 Select three or four short quotations from any works of literature, for instance:

A little learning is a dangerous thing. (Alexander Pope)

No man is an island, entire of itself . . . (John Donne)

(A useful source of further ideas is the *Oxford Dictionary of Quotations*.)

2 Prepare one or more sets of three quotations and make copies for one third of the class.

IN CLASS

1 *Class discussion.* Ask the class to call out the names of some well known public figures and institutions in their city or country. Write these up in separate columns, for instance:

A	B
Ringo Starr	The House of Lords
Barbara Cartland	Manchester United
Peter Ustinov	The RSPCA
Glenda Jackson	The London Stock Exchange

2 Ask the students to work in groups of three. Give them these instructions:

'Imagine that one of the people from column A has been invited to give a speech by one of the institutions in column B. Choose one of the public figures and decide where he or she will speak, and on what occasion. For example, you might decide that Glenda Jackson is going to speak at the opening of a new building for the London Stock Exchange.'

(These British examples are given as illustrations. In the activity, the people and places you choose will more likely be from your own country.)

3 Ask the groups to decide what the most important point in the speech will be. When they have decided, they write out ten or twelve sentences illustrating this point (in English, because many foreign guests have been invited).

4 After about five minutes, give each group a set of three quotations. Ask them to choose any one of the quotations, and to work it into their speech.

5 When the groups are ready, ask one person from each group to deliver their speech to the rest of the class.

VARIATION 1

Instead of giving the students a few short quotations, you can give them one longer text (a sonnet, or a monologue from a play) and leave them free to select any words or lines they wish.

VARIATION 2

Instead of asking one student in each group to deliver the speech, suggest that all three members take part. Each student then speaks a short part of the text they have prepared. This helps to make it more of a joint activity.

(For development of *Variation 2*, see Maley and Duff: *Drama Techniques in Language Learning*.)

NOTES

1 This is a challenging yet most enjoyable activity. It will probably work best if the students are already familiar with approaches such as those suggested in Section 1.

2 Improvisation is an important part of this activity. The students should be given enough time to make a rough draft of the speech, but they should also be ready to speak off the cuff if they are not fully prepared.

3 If you are working with set books, or with textbooks which contain literary passages, you could take sample quotations from passages the students already know. Their familiarity with the words will lend added interest.

SAMPLE TEXTS

1 Some men are born great, some achieve greatness,
and some have greatness thrust upon them.
(Shakespeare: Malvolio in *Twelfth Night*)

2 Water, water, everywhere,
Nor any drop to drink.
(Coleridge: 'The Rime of the Ancient Mariner')

3 A dog starved at his master's gate
Predicts the ruin of the State.
(William Blake: 'Auguries of Innocence')

4 Turning and turning in the widening gyre
The falcon cannot hear the falconer;
Things fall apart; the centre cannot hold;
Mere anarchy is loosed upon the world.
(W. B. Yeats: 'The Second Coming')

5 All the world's a stage,
And all the men and women merely players:
They have their exits and their entrances;
And one man in his time plays many parts.
(Shakespeare: Jaques in *As You Like It*)

6 We need to be able to lose our minds in
order to come to our senses.

2.2 Speculation 2

LEVEL   Intermediate

TIME   15 minutes

PREPARATION   **1** From a novel or short story, select a passage of dialogue which is more or less free from comment by the author. On one sheet, copy out the dialogue (passage 2). On two other sheets, copy out the paragraphs which come before (passage 1) and after the dialogue (passage 3). (See sample texts A and B.)

2 Make enough copies of your texts for one third of the class.

IN CLASS   **1** Ask the students to form groups of three. Give each group a copy of the dialogue (passage 2) in your sample text A. Ask them to deduce what they can about the situation:

– *Who is talking, about whom, where, and why?*

Allow time for the groups to compare impressions.

2 Give the groups copies of the passage which comes before the dialogue (passage 1). Ask them to check their predictions against the text.

3 Before giving out the third passage, ask the students to decide (in this case) how Mary feels about what she has just heard, and whether, for instance, she feels:

angry	indifferent	hurt
bored	surprised	relieved
anxious	disbelieving	jealous
shocked	self-pitying	vengeful

4 To complete the discussion, give the groups copies of passage 3. Which of the words above do they now think are most/least appropriate?

NOTES

1 This is basically a warm-up exercise which could be used to prepare the students for a more extended activity, such as 2.8 *Completing the picture*.

2 *Translation*. An interesting way of extending this activity is to ask the students to translate the dialogue (passage 2) before proceeding to speculate about the situation. After the speculation (*In class*, step 4), ask the students to suggest improvements to their translations of the dialogue.

3 (Optional) *Listening*. Before handing out passages 1 and 3, you may want to play a recording of passage 2 if you are able to obtain one.

4 *Short stories*. The same approach may also be used to introduce students to a short story. An example is given in sample text B.

5 See also the techniques suggested in 2.3 *Storylines 1*.

SAMPLE TEXT A

2 'She's not fifteen any longer: it is ridiculous! Someone should tell her about her clothes'.

'How old is she?'

'Must be well over thirty. She has been going strong for years. She was working long before I began working, and that was a good twelve years ago.'

'Why doesn't she marry? She must have had plenty of chances.'

There was a dry chuckle. 'I don't think so. My husband was keen on her himself once, but he thinks she will never marry. She just isn't like that, isn't like that at all. Something missing somewhere.'

'Oh, I don't know.'

'She's gone off so much, in any case. The other day I caught sight of her in the street and hardly recognized her. It's a fact! The way she plays all those games, her skin is like sandpaper, and she's got so thin.'

'But she's such a nice girl.'

'She'll never set the rivers on fire, though.'

'She'd make someone a good wife. She's a good sort, Mary.'

'She should marry someone years older than herself. A man of fifty would suit her . . . you'll see, she will marry someone old enough to be her father one of these days.'

'One never can tell!'

1 She was in the house of a married friend, sitting on the verandah, with a lighted room behind her. She was alone; and heard people talking in low voices, and caught her own name. She rose to go inside and declare herself: it was typical of her that her first thought was, how unpleasant it would be for her friends to know she had overheard. Then she sank down again, and waited for a suitable moment to pretend she had just come in from the garden. This was the conversation she listened to, while her face burned and her hands went clammy.

-- ✂

3 There was another chuckle, good-hearted enough, but it sounded cruelly malicious to Mary. She was stunned and outraged; but most of all deeply wounded that her friends could discuss her thus. She was so naïve, so unconscious of herself in relation to other people, that it had never entered her head that people could discuss her behind her back. And the things they had said! She sat there writhing, twisting her hands. Then she composed herself and went back into the room to join her treacherous friends, who greeted her as cordially as if they had not just that moment driven knives into her heart and thrown her quite off balance; she could not recognize herself in the picture they had made of her!

(Doris Lessing: *The Grass is Singing*)

SAMPLE TEXT B
2 'What's the letter, darling? I didn't know there had been a post.'
'It's from Josephine. It came yesterday.'
'But you haven't even opened it!' she exclaimed without a word of reproach.
'I don't want to think about her.'
'But, darling, she may be ill.'
'Not she.'
'Or in distress.'
'She earns more with her fashion-designs than I do with my stories.'
'Darling, let's be kind. We can afford to be. We are so happy.'
So he opened the letter. It was affectionate and uncomplaining and he read it with distaste.

-- ✂

1 How wonderfully secure and peaceful a genuine marriage seemed to Carter, when he attained it at the age of forty-two. He even enjoyed every moment of the church service, except when he saw Josephine wiping away a tear as he conducted Julia down the aisle. It was typical of this new frank relationship that Josephine was there at all. He had no secrets from Julia; they had often talked together of his ten tormented years with Josephine, of her extravagant jealously, of her well-timed hysterics. 'It was her insecurity,' Julia argued with understanding, and she was quite convinced that in a little while it would be possible to form a friendship with Josephine.

'I doubt it, darling.'

'Why? I can't help being fond of anyone who loved you.'

'It was a rather cruel love.'

'Perhaps at the end when she knew she was losing you, but, darling, there *were* happy years.'

'Yes.' But he wanted to forget that he had ever loved anyone before Julia.

Her generosity sometimes staggered him. On the seventh day of their honeymoon, when they were drinking retsina in a little restaurant on the beach by Sunium, he accidentally took a letter from Josephine out of his pocket. It had arrived the day before and he had concealed it, for fear of hurting Julia. It was typical of Josephine that she could not leave him alone for the brief period of the honeymoon. Even her handwriting was now abhorrent to him – very neat, very small, in black ink the colour of her hair. Julia was platinum-fair. How had he ever thought that black hair was beautiful? Or been impatient to read letters in black ink?

3 Dear Philip, I didn't want to be a death's head at the reception, so I had no chance to say goodbye and wish you both the greatest possible happiness. I thought Julia looked terribly beautiful and so very, very young. You must look after her carefully. I know how well you can do that , Philip dear. When I saw her, I couldn't help wondering why you took such a long time to make up your mind to leave me. Silly Philip. It's much less painful to act quickly.

I don't suppose you are interested to hear about my activities now, but just in case you are worrying a little about me – you know what an old worrier you are – I want you to know that I'm working *very* hard at a whole series for – guess, the French *Vogue*. They are paying me a fortune in francs, and I simply have no time for unhappy thoughts. I've been back once – I hope you don't mind – to our apartment (slip of the tongue) because I'd lost a key sketch. I found it at the back of our communal drawer – the ideas-bank, do you remember? I thought I'd taken all my stuff away, but there it was between the leaves of the story you started that heavenly summer, and never finished, at Napoule. Now I'm rambling on when all I really wanted to say was: Be happy both of you. Love, Josephine.

Carter handed the letter to Julia and said, 'It could have been worse.'

'But would she like me to read it?'

(Graham Greene: 'Mortmain', from *May we Borrow your Husband?*)

--✄

2.3 Storylines 1

LEVEL   **Intermediate to advanced**

TIME   **20 – 25 minutes**

PREPARATION   1 Choose a short story or a chapter from a novel (approximately fifteen pages). From each page of the story, select one or two key sentences; that is, ones which give an indication of the storyline. Write out these sentences in order and make them up into a task sheet. (See sample text.) If you wish to make the activity slightly easier, you could also add the opening paragraph and the ending.

2 Make enough copies of your task sheet for one third of the class.

IN CLASS   1 Ask the students to work in groups of three. Give each group a copy of your task sheet. The students discuss what they think happens in the story, and find a possible explanation for each of the sentences.

2 After discussion (ten minutes), the groups compare their different versions of the story.

3 *Class discussion.* Ask the class to call out those sentences from the story which they found most difficult to explain. Let them compare their suggestions. Finally, reveal what actually happened in the story.

NOTES

1 This activity helps to overcome one of the main difficulties of working with literature in class: how to deal with longer texts. Here, the students are in a sense skimming through a longer text which they may later read on their own. You will find that the interest aroused is usually great and that, by the end of the activity, the students actually want to read the whole text. This eagerness to know what happens is not easily aroused when students are simply asked to plod through the text page by page.

2 Although the activity is best suited to unfamiliar material, it can also be used as a form of memory test to refresh familiar texts, and it is particularly suitable for revising set works or texts which may feature in examinations.

VARIATION

This activity can also be done orally throughout.

IN CLASS

1 Read the selected sentences aloud to the whole class.

2 Then read the opening paragraph and the first of the selected sentences. Ask the students to suggest what is happening. Then go on to the second of the sentences. Continue in the same way through to the end.

In the oral variation, you could try giving the students longer fragments from the story.

SAMPLE TEXT

Poison

Opening

It must have been around midnight when I drove home, and as I approached the gates of the bungalow I switched off the headlamps of the car so the beam wouldn't swing in through the window of the side bedroom and wake Harry Pope. But I needn't have bothered. Coming up the drive I noticed his light was still on, so he was awake anyway – unless perhaps he'd dropped off while reading.

Fragments

1   I could see he was awake. But he didn't move.

2   'For God's sake don't make a noise. Take your shoes off before you come nearer . . .'

3   He was wearing a pair of pyjamas with blue, brown and white stripes, and he was sweating terribly.

4   'What is it, Harry . . . Oh, my God! . . . How long ago?'

5   'Small, about ten inches.'

6 'Hours,' he whispered. 'Hours and bloody hours and hours.'

7 . . . and fetched a small sharp knife from the kitchen. I put it in my pocket ready to use instantly in case something went wrong while we were still thinking out a plan.

8 'Dr Ganderbai,' I said . . . 'Look, could you come round at once?'

9 . . . he walked across the floor noiselessly, delicately, like a careful cat.

10 'Intravenously.'

11 'Is he safe now?' I asked.
   'No.'

12 'Chloroform,' he said suddenly 'Ordinary chloroform. That is best. Now quick!' He took me my arm and pulled me towards the balcony. 'Drive to my house!'

13 I do not know how long it took him to slide that tube in a few inches. It may have been twenty minutes, it may have been forty. I never once saw the tube move. I knew it was going in because the visible part of it grew gradually shorter.

14 Harry lay there twitching his mouth, sweating, closing his eyes, opening them, looking at me, at the ceiling, at me again, but never at Ganderbai.

15 Then I saw the white cord of his pyjamas . . . a little further and I saw a button, a mother-of-pearl button . . . I distinctly remember thinking about Harry being very refined when I saw that button.

16 'Mr Pope, you are of course *quite* sure you saw it in the first place?' There was a note of sarcasm in Ganderbai's voice that he would never have employed in ordinary circumstances.

17 'Are you telling me I'm a liar?' he shouted.

Ending

'All he needs is a good holiday', he said quietly, without looking at me, then he started the engine and drove off.

(Roald Dahl: 'Poison')

2.4 Storylines 2: suspense

LEVEL   **Intermediate**

TIME   **45 – 60 minutes**

PREPARATION   1 For this activity, select a passage from a novel in which the suspense is gradually built up to a climax. The passage should preferably contain an even mixture of dialogue and descriptive prose.

2 Choose certain key points in the text, and blank out the words. (Your cuts should not be longer than five or six words, at most.)

3 Give each student a copy of the text to read out of class. While they read it at home, they should think of possible words to complete the gaps.

IN CLASS   1 Ask the students to work in groups of three or four, and to discuss their various suggestions for the wording of the blank spaces. Set a time-limit of twenty minutes for this part of the activity.

2 *Class discussion.* Ask the class to call out their best suggestions for each of the blank spaces. If there are any errors of language, correct these on the spot. Then reveal to the class the original wording for each space.

NOTES   1 This activity combines several of the approaches already described, including speculation, suggesting the words, and character descriptions. It also complements certain other activities, such as 2.3 *Storylines 1* and 4.1 and 4.3 *Focus on language*.

2 Suspense, in literature, is often built up by holding the reader back, that is, by deliberately slowing down the story through the introduction of detail or through asides. For instance:

I had mechanically turned in this latter direction, and was strolling along the lonely high-road – idly wondering, I remember , what the Cumberland young ladies would look like – when, in one moment, every drop of blood in my body was brought to a stop by the touch of a hand laid lightly and suddenly on my shoulder from behind me.

I turned on the instant, with my fingers tightening round the handle of my stick.

There, in the middle of the broad, bright high-road – there, as if it had that moment sprung out of the earth or dropped from the heaven – stood the figure of a solitary woman dressed from head to foot in white . . .

When preparing for this activity, it is important *not* to cut out this detail (though you may, of course, shorten the text in other ways). It is also important to give the students time to 'get into' the passage: this is why we suggest that the initial reading be done out of class.

3 In selecting the words to be omitted (the blank spaces), you may wish to tell the students exactly how many words are missing, or to offer a clue to the wording. For instance:

a) (2) . . . ? she said, still quietly and rapidly.
b) (2) . . . ? she said, still quietly and rapidly. (4 words)
c) (2) (hear) . . . ? she said, still quietly and rapidly.

The approach suggested under c) is particularly useful if you wish to draw attention to a particular language structure, say, the difference between: '*Do you hear me?*', '*Have you heard me?*', '*Can you hear me?*', '*Did you hear me?*', and so on. It also helps to bring out any incorrect usages, such as '*Are you hearing me?*'

4 You will notice that, in the sample text, we have concentrated more on the everyday use of language (*Quite sure*, *Why do you ask?*, *Do you live in London?*), and that we have given little attention to so-called literary expressions such as: '. . . dressed from head to foot *in white garments*', or '. . . her face *bent in grave inquiry*'. These are expressions which, in our opinion, the students do not need to imitate or actively reproduce; passive understanding is all that is required.

In devising your own version of a text such as this, you may find it helpful to distinguish between two kinds of blank spaces:

a. those which test *language skill*:
(3) I asked *if that was* the way to London. (reported speech)
(6) Tell me how I can help you, and *if I can, I will*. (use of tenses with *if*-clause)

b. those which test *reading comprehension*:
(9) Do you *know many people in London?*
    Yes, a great many.
    Many men of rank and title?

Here, the missing words in the question (*know many people in London*) can be inferred from the responses which follow:
'Yes, a great many . . . Many men of rank and title?'

SAMPLE TEXT

The Woman in White

(In the passage below, the narrator (*I*) is walking back to his home in London, after a meeting at which he has agreed to teach painting to the two daughters of Mr Fairlie, of Limmeridge House, Cumberland, in northern England. On his way home, he has a strange meeting.)

The heat had been painfully oppressive all day, and it was now a close and sultry night. I walked forward a few paces on the shortest way back to London, then stopped and hestitated.

The moon was full and broad in the dark blue starless sky, and the broken ground of the heath looked wild enough in the mysterious light to be hundreds of miles away from the great city that lay beneath it. The idea of descending any sooner than I could help into the heat and gloom of London repelled me. The prospect of going to bed in my airless chambers, and the prospect of gradual suffocation, seemed, in my present restless frame of mind and body, to be one and the same thing. I determined to stroll home in the purer air by the most roundabout way I could take; to follow the white winding paths across the lonely heath; and to approach London through its most open suburb by striking into the Finchley Road, and so getting back, in the cool of the new morning, by the western side of Regent's Park.

By the time I had arrived at the end of the road I had become completely absorbed in my own fanciful visions of Limmeridge House, of Mr Fairlie, and of the two ladies whose practice in the art of water-colour painting I was so soon to superintend.

I had now arrived at that particular point of my walk where four roads met – the road to Hampstead, along which I had returned, the road to Finchley, the road to the West End, and the road back to London. I had mechanically turned in this latter direction, and was strolling along the lonely high-road – idly wondering, I remember, what the Cumberland young ladies would look like – when, in one moment, every drop of blood in my body was brought to a stop by the touch of a hand laid lightly and suddenly on my shoulder from behind me.

I turned on the instant, with my fingers tightening round the handle of my stick.

There, in the middle of the broad, bright high-road – there, as if it had that moment sprung out of the earth or dropped from the heaven – stood the figure of a solitary woman, dressed from head to foot in white garments, her face bent in grave inquiry on mine, her hand pointing to the dark cloud over London, as I faced her.

I was far too seriously startled by the suddenness with which this extraordinary apparition stood before me, in the dead of night and in that lonely place, to ask what she wanted. The strange woman spoke first.

'(1) . . .?' she said.

I looked attentively at her, as she put that singular question to me. It was then nearly one o'clock. All I could discern distinctly by the moonlight was a colourless, youthful face, meagre and sharp to look at about the cheeks and chin; large, grave, wistfully attentive eyes; nervous, uncertain lips; and light hair of a pale, brownish-yellow hue. There was nothing wild, nothing immodest in her manner: it was quiet and self-controlled, a little melancholy and a little touched by suspicion; not exactly the manner of a lady, and, at the same time, not the manner of a woman in the humblest rank of life. The voice, little as I had yet heard of it, had something curiously still and mechanical in its tones, and the utterance was remarkably rapid. She held a small bag in her hand: and her dress – bonnet, shawl, and gown all of white – was, so far as I could guess, certainly not composed of very delicate or very expensive materials. Her figure was slight, and rather above the average height – her gait and actions free from the slightest approach to extravagance. This was all that I could observe of her in the dim light and under the perplexingly strange circumstances of our meeting. What sort of a woman she was, and how she came to be out alone in the high-road, an hour after midnight, I altogether failed to guess. The one thing of which I felt certain was, that the grossest of mankind could not have misconstrued her motive in speaking, even at that suspiciously late hour and in that suspiciously lonely place.

'(2) . . . ?' she said, still quietly and rapidly, and without the least fretfulness or impatience. 'I asked (3) . . . the way to London.'

'Yes.' I replied, 'that is the way: it leads to St John's Wood and the Regent's Park. You must excuse my not answering you before. I was rather startled by your sudden appearance in the road; and I am, even now, quite unable to account for it.'

'You don't suspect me of doing anything wrong, do you? (4) . . . . I have met with an accident – I am very unfortunate in being here alone so late. Why do you suspect me of doing wrong?'

She spoke with unnecessary earnestness and agitation, and shrank back from me several paces. I did my best to reassure her.

'Pray don't suppose that I have any idea of suspecting you,' I said, 'or any other wish than to be of assistance to you, if I can. I only wondered at your appearance in the road, because it seemed to me to be empty the instant before I saw you.'

She turned, and pointed back to a place at the junction of the road to London and the road to Hampstead, where there was a gap in the hedge.

'I heard you coming.' she said, 'and hid there to see what (5) . . ., before I risked speaking. I doubted and feared about it till you passed; and then I was obliged to steal after you, and touch you.'

Steal after me and touch me? Why not call to me? Strange, to say the least of it.

'May I trust you?' she asked. 'You don't think the worse of me because I have met with an accident?' She stopped in confusion; shifted her bag from one hand to the other; and sighed bitterly.

The loneliness and helplessness of the woman touched me. The natural impulse to assist her and to spare her got the better of the judgement, the caution, the worldly tact, which an older, wiser, and colder man might have summoned to help him in this strange emergency.

'You may trust me for any harmless purposes,' I said. 'If it troubles you to explain your strange situation to me, don't think of returning to the subject again. I have no right to ask you for any explanations. Tell me how I can help you; and (6) . . .'

'You are very kind, and I am very, very thankful (7) . . . .' The first touch of womanly tenderness that I had heard from her trembled in her voice as she said the words: but no tears glistened in those large, wistfully attentive eyes of hers, which were still fixed on me. 'I have only been in London once before,' she went on, more and more rapidly, 'and I know nothing about that side of it, yonder. Can I get a carriage of any kind? Is it too late? I don't know. If you could show me where to get a carriage – and if you will only promise not to interfere with me, and to let me leave you, when and how I please – I have a friend in London who will be glad to receive me – I want nothing else – will you promise?'

She looked anxiously up and down the road; shifted her bag again from one hand to the other; repeated the words, 'Will you promise?' and looked hard in my face, with a pleading fear and confusion that it troubled me to see.

What could I do? Here was a stranger utterly and helplessly at my mercy – and that stranger a forlorn woman. No house was near; no one was passing whom I could consult; and no earthly right existed on my part to give me a power of control over her, even if I had known how to exercise it. What could I do?

What I did do, was to try and gain time by questioning her.

'Are you sure that your friend in London will receive you at such a late hour as this?' I said.

'(8) . . . . Only say you will let me leave you when and how I please – only say you won't interfere with me. Will you promise?'

As she repeated the words for the third time, she came close to me and laid her hand, with a sudden gentle stealthiness, on my bosom – a thin hand; a cold hand (when I removed it with mine) even on that sultry night. Remember that I was young; remember that the hand which touched me was a woman's.

'Will you promise?'

'Yes.'

One word! The little familiar word that is on everybody's lips, every hour in the day. Oh me! and I tremble, now, when I write it.

We set our faces towards London, and walked on together in the first still hour of the new day – I, and this woman, whose name, whose character, whose story, whose very presence by my side, at that moment, were fathomless mysteries to me. It was like a dream. It was her voice again that first broke the silence between us.

'I want to ask you something,' she said suddenly. 'Do you (9) . . .?

'Yes, a great many.'

'Many men of rank and title?' There was an unmistakable tone of suspicion in the strange question. I hesitated about answering it.

'Some,' I said, after a moment's silence.

'Many' – she came to a full stop, and looked me searchingly in the face – 'many men of the rank of Baronet?'

Too much astonished to reply, I questioned her in my turn.

'(10) . . .?'

'Because I hope, for my own sake, there is one Baronet that you don't know.'

'Will you tell me his name?'

'I can't – I daren't – I forget myself when I mention it.' She spoke loudly and almost fiercely, raised her clenched hand in the air, and shook it passionately; then, on a sudden, controlled herself again, and added, in tones lowered to a whisper, 'Tell me which of them *you* know.'

I mentioned three names. Two, the names of fathers of families whose daughters I taught; one, the name of a bachelor who had once taken me on a cruise in his yacht, to make sketches for him.

'Ah! you *don't* know him,' she said, with a sigh of relief. 'Are you a man of rank and title yourself?'

'Far from it. I am only a drawing-master.'

As the reply passed my lips – a little bitterly, perhaps – she took my arm with the abruptness which characterised all her actions.

'Not a man of rank and title,' she repeated to herself. 'Thank God! I may trust *him*.'

I had hitherto contrived to master my curiosity out of consideration for my companion; but it got the better of me now.

'I am afraid you have serious reason to complain of some man of rank and title?' I said. 'I am afraid the baronet, whose name you are unwilling to mention to me, has done you some grievous wrong? Is he the cause of your being out here at this strange time of night?'

'Don't ask me; don't make me talk of it,' she answered. 'I'm not fit now. I have been cruelly used and cruelly wronged. You will be kinder than ever, if you will walk on fast, and not speak to me. I sadly want to quiet myself, if I can.'

We moved forward again at a quick pace; and for half an hour, at least, not a word passed on either side. From time to time, being forbidden to make any more inquiries, I stole a look at her face. It was always the same; the lips close shut, the brow frowning, the eyes looking straight forward, eagerly and yet absently. We had reached the first houses before her set features relaxed, and she spoke once more.

(11) . . . ? she said.

'Yes.' As I answered, it struck me that she might have formed some intention of appealing to me for assistance or advice, and that I ought to spare her a possible disappointment by warning her of my approaching absence from home. So I added, 'But tomorrow I shall be away from London for some time. I am going into the country.'

'Where?' she asked. 'North or south?'

'North – to Cumberland.'

'Cumberland!' she repeated the word tenderly. 'Ah! I wish I was going there too. I was once happy in Cumberland.'

I tried again to lift the veil that hung between this woman and me.

(12) . . .,' I said, 'in the beautiful Lake country.'

'No,' she answered, 'I was born in Hampshire; but I once went to school for a little while in Cumberland. Lakes? I don't remember any lakes. It's Limmeridge village, and Limmeridge House, I should like to see again.'

It was my turn now to stop suddenly. In the excited state of my curiosity, at that moment, the chance reference to Mr Fairlie's place of residence, on the lips of my strange companion, staggered me with astonishment.

'Did you hear anybody calling after us?' she asked, looking up and down the road affrightedly, the instant I stopped.

'No, no. I was only struck by the name of Limmeridge House. I heard it mentioned by some Cumberland people a few days since.'

'Ah! not *my* people. Mrs Fairlie is dead; and her husband is dead;
and their little girl may be married and gone away by this time, I
can't say who lives at Limmeridge now. If any more are left there of
that name, I only know I love them for Mrs Fairlie's sake.'

She seemed about to say more; but while she was speaking, we
came within view of the turnpike, at the top of the Avenue Road.
Her hand tightened round my arm, and she looked anxiously at the
gate before us.

'Is the turnpike man looking out?' she asked.

He was not looking out; no one else was near the place when we
passed through the gate. The sight of the gas-lamps and houses
seemed to agitate her, and to make her impatient.

'This is London,' she said. 'Do you see any carriage I can get? I
am (13) . . . . I want to (14) . . . and be driven away.'

I explained to her that we must walk a little further to get to a
cab-stand, unless we were fortunate enough to meet with an empty
vehicle; and then tried to resume the subject of Cumberland. It was
useless. That idea of shutting herself in, and being driven away,
had now got full possession of her mind. She could think and talk of
nothing else.

We had hardly proceeded a third of the way down the Avenue
Road when I saw a cab draw up at a house a few doors below us, on
the opposite side of the way. A gentleman got out and let himself in
at the garden door. I hailed the cab, as the driver mounted the box
again. When we crossed the road, my companion's impatience
increased to such an extent that she almost forced me to run.

'It's so late,' she said. 'I am only in a hurry because it's so late.'

'I can't take you, sir, if you're not going towards Tottenham
Court Road,' said the driver civilly, when I opened the cab door.
'My horse is dead beat, and I can't get him no further than the
stable.'

'Yes, yes. That will do for me. I'm going that way – I'm going
that way.' She spoke with breathless eagerness, and pressed by me
into the cab.

I had assured myself that the man was sober as well as civil before
I let her enter the vehicle. And now, when she was seated inside, I
entreated her to let me see her set down safely at her destination.

'No, no, no,' she said vehemently. 'I'm quite safe, and quite
happy now. If you are a gentleman, (15) . . . . Let him drive on till
I stop him. Thank you – oh! thank you, thank you!'

My hand was on the cab door. She caught it in hers, kissed it,
and pushed it away. The cab drove off at the same moment –
I started into the road, with some vague idea of stopping it again, I
hardly knew why – hesitated from dread of frightening and
distressing her – called, at last, but not loudly enough to attract the
driver's attention. The sound of the wheels grew fainter in the
distance – the cab melted into the black shadows on the road – the
woman in white (16) . . . .

Ten minutes or more had passed. I was still on the same side of
the way; now mechanically walking forward a few paces; now
stopping again absently. At one moment I found myself doubting

the reality of my own adventure; at another I was perplexed and distressed by an uneasy sense of having done wrong, which yet left me confusedly ignorant of how I could have done right. I hardly knew where I was going, or (17) . . . . I was conscious of nothing but the confusion of my own thoughts, when I was abruptly recalled to myself – awakened, I might almost say – by the sound of rapidly approaching wheels close behind me.

I was on the dark side of the road, in the thick shadow of some garden trees, when I stopped to look round. On the opposite and lighter side of the way, a short distance below me, a policeman was strolling along in the direction of the Regent's Park.

The carriage passed me – an open chaise driven by two men.

'Stop!' cried one. 'There's a policeman. Let's ask him.'

The horse was instantly pulled up, a few yards beyond the dark place where I stood.

'Policeman!' cried the first speaker. 'Have you (18) . . .?'

'What sort of woman, sir?'

'A woman in a lavender-coloured gown –'

'No, no,' interposed the second man. 'The clothes we gave her were found on her bed. She must have gone away in the clothes she wore when she came to us. In white, policeman. A woman in white.'

'I haven't seen her, sir.'

'If you or any of your men meet with the woman, stop her, and send her in careful keeping to that address. I'll pay all expenses, and a fair reward into the bargain.'

The policeman looked at the card that was handed down to him.

'Why are we to stop her, sir? (19) . . . ?'

'Done! She has (20) . . . . Don't forget; a woman in white. Drive on.'

(Wilkie Collins: *The Woman in White*)

KEY	Original wording:

1	Is that the road to London?	11	Do you live in London?
2	Did you hear me?	12	Perhaps you were born . . .
3	. . . if that was . . .	13	. . . tired and frightened . . .
4	I have done nothing wrong.	14	. . . shut myself in . . .
5	. . . sort of man you were . . .	15	. . . remember your promise.
6	. . . if I can, I will.	16	. . . was gone.
7	. . . to have met you.	17	. . . what I meant to do next.
8	Quite sure.	18	. . . seen a woman pass this way?
9	. . . know many people in London?	19	What has she done?
10	Why do you ask?	20	. . . escaped from my Asylum.

2.5 Matching texts

LEVEL   Intermediate

TIME   20 – 25 minutes

PREPARATION   1 Find two or three short passages of prose or poetry which could be compared or contrasted. The texts you choose should have certain features in common. For instance, they might deal with different aspects of the same theme, be similar in style or form (monologues, letters, speeches), have similar or identical titles, and so on.

2 Make copies of both texts for the whole class. Your preparation for the *In class* work will, of course, depend on the texts you have chosen. Below we describe an approach which could be used with two poems with the same title 'The Lesson'. (See sample texts.)

IN CLASS   1 *Warm-up discussion.* Ask the students to think back for a few minutes over their own lives, and to recall any incident which left a deep impression on them, and from which they or someone else learnt a lesson. What was the incident? And what was the lesson?

2 Now ask the students to form groups of four and to describe to each other the incident they have in mind.

3 Tell the students that they are going to be working with two short poems, both with the same title 'The Lesson'. Read one of the poems aloud (or play a recording of it). Ask the students to recall any words or lines they can remember. Do the same again using the other poem.

4 Hand out copies of the two poems to all the students. Ask them to work for a few minutes on their own, and to mark:

a. any words or lines that are difficult to understand
b. any words or images they find particularly striking
c. any thoughts or comments that are similar in the two poems.

5 Now ask the students to rearrange themselves in groups of three, and to compare and discuss the lines they have marked.

6 (Optional) *Class discussion.* Two questions you could ask to extend the discussion are:
– *Why are both poems called 'The Lesson'?*
– *Does either of the poems remind you of anything that has happened to you, or to someone you know?*

NOTES   1 The warm-up discussion is an important part of this activity. Firstly, because it helps to put the students in the right frame of mind for working with the poems. Secondly, because it is in itself an exercise in contrast and comparison. An incident which happened in one student's life will often remind others of similar incidents in their own lives.

2 One of the difficulties you may encounter in using matching texts is that, although the two passages clearly have features in common, this fact alone does not necessarily generate discussion. It is usually easier to see the similarities than to explain them.

This is why, in step 3 of *In class*, we focus first on the students' reaction to the words. Ask questions such as:

– *What lines do you find difficult to understand?*
– *What images do you find striking?*

By thinking about such questions, the students gradually come to see in what ways the poems are similar or different. For instance, the line:

. . . Somewhere in myself,
Pride, like a goldfish, flashed a sudden fin.

may for one student be difficult to understand, while another student might find the image striking. Their discussion will lead to the questions:

– *Why is he proud?*
– *Is there a suggestion of pride in the other poem?*
– *Is there a suggestion of shame?*

3 The technique of matching or contrasting texts will be further developed in Section 3 (3.4–3.5 *Discussion topics*).

SAMPLE TEXTS   **The Lesson**

How we laughed!
The old man coughing
All his life away
With asthma. Stumbling
Up the steps ('Poor fool!')
To call the register;
In a world where we knew all
And yet were learning still.
"Get in the pension queue!"
Someone said (me, perhaps).
But stilled we were,
And all in awe
When he lapsed silent,
Head upon the desk.
('Poor old bugger!') Then
Came the ambulance and
All the inquisition fuss
Before we breezed late
Into the next one's class,
Full of new learning
From his sudden lesson.

(David A. Hill)

The Lesson

'Your father's gone,' my bald headmaster said.
His shiny dome and brown tobacco jar
Splintered at once in tears. It wasn't grief.
I cried for knowledge which was bitterer
Than any grief. For there and then I knew
That grief has uses – that a father dead
Could bind the bully's fist a week or two;
And then I cried for shame, then for relief.

I was a month past ten when I learnt this:
I still remember how the noise was stilled
In school-assembly when my grief came in.
Some goldfish in a bowl quietly sculled
Around their shining prison on its shelf.
They were indifferent. All the other eyes
Were turned towards me. Somewhere in myself
Pride, like a goldfish, flashed a sudden fin.

(Edward Lucie-Smith)

2.6 Character sketches

LEVEL	**Intermediate**
TIME	**40 – 60 minutes**
PREPARATION	**1** Compile a selection of short character sketches from different novels or short stories.

2 Prepare sufficient copies of the passages for each group of four students to have one set of four or five texts each. (For suggestions, see sample texts.)

3 Draw up a list of stimulus questions for class discussion after they have read the texts. The questions should be designed to get the students to look back to the text for possible clues. If you ask, for instance:

– *Which of the characters might be a spy?*

the response might be:

– *Richard Pratt*, because he is 'president of a small society' of people who are probably rich and influential.
– *Leamas*, because he looks like a man who is 'not quite a gentleman', and who would not be mistaken for a member in a London club, though he would be given the best table in a Berlin nightclub.
– *Sophie Graveney*, because she has contacts with 'the London embassy'.

Below are two sets of suggestions for the prompt questions:

General

– In your opinion, which of the characters would:

1 lend you £10 if you urgently needed money?
2 regularly go to bed by 22.30 at the latest?
3 usually travel first class?
4 rarely read a newspaper?
5 occasionally go to a football match?
6 enjoy dancing, and dance well?
7 have many foreign stamps in his/her passport?
8 talk very slowly, or very quickly? often, or rarely use hand gestures?
9 keep a cat or dog at home?
10 have a printed visiting card, or notepaper with a printed letterhead?
11 frequently suffer from headaches?
12 do gymnastics in the morning?
    etc.

Specific

– Each of the remarks below was made by one of the characters described. Who said what? For each remark, suggest the most likely speaker.

1 'It's bloody rude.'
2 'I don't like conversations about Life.'
3 'Mrs Goddard, what say you to *half* a glass of wine? A small half glass, put into a tumbler of water?'
4 'We must never fear what is our duty.'
5 'My life's a bit fraught at the moment.'
6 'I'm perfectly willing to bet.'
7 'Don't interrupt. Just damn well wait till I've finished, do you mind?'
8 'I am not concerned with your gratitude to me. There is One Above who has a prior claim.'
9 'He rageth and again he rageth, because he knows his time is short.'
10 'I assume, then, that it's from one of the smaller vineyards?'
12 'An egg boiled very soft is not unwholesome.'

KEY			
1 Sophie Graveney	5 Sophie Graveney	9 Joanna Childe	
2 Leamas	6 Richard Pratt	10 Richard Pratt	
3 Mr Woodhouse	7 Leamas	11 Sophie Graveney	
4 Mrs Poulteney	8 Mrs Poulteney	12 Mr Woodhouse	

IN CLASS

1 *Warm-up discussion.* Ask the students to form groups of four or five. Write up on the board or OHP three column headings:

Speech	Clothes	Mannerisms

Under each column, ask the students to list anything that disturbs them or that they dislike in other people's appearance or behaviour, for instance:

Speech

(I don't like) people who say: 'Have a nice day!', or 'Super', or 'Correct me if I'm wrong'; people who whisper in public, talk with their hand in front of their mouth, don't finish their sentences, or sneeze loudly.

Clothes

people who wear T-shirts with advertising slogans; men or women who wear sunglasses indoors; women who wear fur coats with jeans; men who wear tracksuits, and don't run.

Mannerisms

people who click ballpoints, jingle coins in their pockets, keep looking at their watch, yawn when you're talking, or take their shoes off in the train.

2 The groups exchange notes and discuss points of disagreement.

3 *Discussion based on the texts.* The students remain in the groups they have already formed. Give each group copies of four of the character sketches. (See sample texts.) Allow time for silent reading, then ask the students to discuss among themselves their first impressions of the characters.

4 (Optional) Write up a few adjectives to stimulate discussion, for instance:
– *Do any of the following words apply to the characters you have been reading about?*

sly	*warm*	*reserved*
cynical	*timid*	*pompous*
naïve	*trustworthy*	*dull*

5 While the students are discussing, write up or display the questions you have prepared. (See *Preparation*, step 3.) Give the groups at least ten minutes to discuss their own reactions. Then round off the activity with a class discussion which could include talking about the portraits at the end of this activity, in which case ask the students:
– *Do any of the people in the pictures resemble any of the characters you have just read about? If so, in what way?*
– *How do the portraits differ from the image of the characters you had formed from your reading?*

1 People are the life-blood of literature. And we react to these people, the characters of fiction, much in the same way as we react to people in everyday life. We love them, hate them, suspect them, admire them – and want to talk about them.

This is why the activity begins with a fairly long introductory exercise, which draws exclusively on the students' personal feelings about other people. In discussing the give-away details of speech, appearance, and mannerisms in people they have already met, the students are also preparing to talk about people they have not yet met, that is, the characters of fiction.

2 Selecting material for this activity should be no problem. Literature abounds in character descriptions. It is important, however, to remember that the aim of the activity is to deduce rather than to describe. The students are not being asked (as they often are) to 'Describe the character in your own words'. Instead, they are being asked to deduce, from clues in the text, what the person might be like.

Clearly, the students' personal impressions will differ. These differences will come out in their responses to the general questions in *Preparation*, step 3. Here, you may allow plenty of room for disagreement. But in dealing with the specific questions, you should be more rigorous, and ask the students to look for some connection between the dialogue fragments and details mentioned in the descriptive texts. Here are some examples of the clues that could be picked up:

a. Description (Mrs Poulteney)
    Mrs Poulteney had two obsessions. One was Dirt and the other was Immorality . . . Failure to be seen at church on Sunday was tantamount to proof of the worst moral laxity.

    Dialogue fragment
    'I am not concerned with your gratitude to me. There is One Above who has a prior claim.'

b. Description (Leamas)
    He looked like a man who could make trouble, a man who looked after his money, a man who was not quite a gentleman.

    Dialogue fragment
    'Don't interrupt. Just damn well wait till I've finished, do you mind?'

c. Description (Joanna Childe)
    Joanna Childe had been drawn to this profession by her good voice and love of poetry . . . poetry, especially the declamatory sort, excited and possessed her.

    Dialogue fragment
    'He rageth and again he rageth, because he knows his time is short.'

In each case, there is a clear link between what is mentioned in the description and what is said in the remark, for example: *He looked like a man who could make trouble* and 'Don't interrupt. Just wait till I've finished.'

But it must be stressed that here, as in all the speculation activities, what the students should be looking for is a plausible response. The 'right answer' can be given later.

SOURCES

1 Paul Theroux: *The London Embassy*
2 John Le Carré: *The Spy Who Came in from the Cold*
3 Muriel Spark: *The Girls of Slender Means*
4 Roald Dahl: 'Taste', in the collection of stories *Someone Like You*
5 John Fowles: *The French Lieutenant's Woman*
6 Jane Austen: *Emma*

SAMPLE TEXTS

1 Sophie Graveney

The fashion in London that year was rags – expensive ones but rags all the same. Women wore torn blouses and patched jeans. Their hair was cut in a raggedy way – front hanks of it dyed pink and green and bright orange and blue. It was a popular look, but it was not easy to achieve. It took imagination, and time, and a great deal of money for these spoiled wealthy girls to appear down and out.

But Sophie Graveney wore a smooth blouse of light silk the texture of skin and a close-fitting skirt slit all the way to her hip. She said she could not bear to be mistaken for someone poor, and was willing to risk being called unfashionable for her rich clothes . . . People stared at Sophie. She was no punk. Horton, my boss at the London embassy, had called her 'an English rose'.

2 Leamas

Leamas was a short man with close, iron–grey hair, and the physique of a swimmer. He was very strong . . . He had a utilitarian approach to clothes, as he did to most other things, and even the spectacles he occasionally wore had steel rims. Most of his suits were of artificial fibre, none of them had waistcoats. He favoured shirts of the American kind, with buttons on the points.

It was hard to place Leamas. If he were to walk into a London club the porter would certainly not mistake him for a member; in a Berlin night-club they usually gave him the best table. He looked like a man who could make trouble, a man who looked after his money, a man who was not quite a gentleman.

The air hostess thought he was interesting.

3 Joanna Childe

Joanna Childe was a daughter of a country rector. She had a good intelligence and strong obscure emotions. She was training to be a teacher of elocution and, while attending a school of drama, already had pupils of her own. Joanna Childe had been drawn to this profession by her good voice and love of poetry which she loved rather as it might be assumed a cat loves birds; poetry, especially the declamatory sort, excited and possessed her; she would pounce on the stuff, play with it quivering in her mind, and when she had got it by heart, she spoke it forth with devouring relish. Mostly, she indulged the habit while giving elocution lessons at the club where she was highly thought of for it. The vibrations of Joanna's elocution voice from the room where she frequently rehearsed were felt to add tone and style to the establishment when boy-friends called.

4 Richard Pratt

There were six of us to dinner that night at Mike Schofield's house in London: Mike and his wife and daughter, my wife and I, and a man called Richard Pratt.

Richard Pratt was a famous gourmet. He was president of a small society known as the Epicures, and each month he circulated privately to its members a pamphlet on food and wines. He organized dinners where sumptuous dishes and rare wines were served. He refused to smoke for fear of harming his palate, and when discussing a wine, he had a curious habit of referring to it as though it were a living being. 'A prudent wine,' he would say. Or, 'A good-humoured wine, benevolent and cheerful – slightly obscene, perhaps, but none the less good-humoured.'

5 Mrs Poulteney

Mrs Poulteney had two obsessions. One was Dirt, and the other was Immorality. In neither field did anything untoward escape her eagle eye. She was like some plump vulture, endlessly circling in her endless leisure, and endowed with a miraculous sixth sense as regards dust, finger-marks, insufficiently starched linen, smells, stains, breakages and all the ills that houses are heir to. But the most abominable thing of all was that even outside her house she acknowledged no bounds to her authority. Failure to be seen at church on Sunday was tantamount to proof of the worst moral laxity.

6 Mr Woodhouse

Mr Woodhouse was fond of society in his own way. He liked very much to have his friends come and see him; and from various united causes, from his long residence at Hartfield, and his good nature, from his fortune, his house, and his daughter, he could command the visits of his own little circle, in a great measure, as he liked. He had not much intercourse with any families beyond that circle; his horror of late hours, and large dinner-parties, made him unfit for any acquaintance but such as would visit him on his own terms . . . Upon such occasions poor Mr. Woodhouse's feelings were in sad warfare. He loved to have the cloth laid, because it had been the fashion of his youth, but his conviction of suppers being very unwholesome made him rather sorry to see anything put on it; and while his hospitality would have welcomed his visitors to everything, his care for their health made him grieve that they would eat.

2.7 Suggesting the words

LEVEL

Lower intermediate to advanced

TIME

15 – 20 minutes

PREPARATION

1 For this activity, you will need passages of twenty to thirty lines involving dialogue between two characters. The extracts should as far as possible be self-explanatory. That is, the students should be able to understand them without needing much explanation of the context.

From the dialogue in the passage(s), select eight to ten short remarks, such as '*I'd like that*', '*Do you mind?*', or fragments of remarks like '. . . *driving away*', '. . . *get some sleep*'. Then write out the passage(s), omitting the selected expressions.

If you think it necessary, write a brief summary to give the students a guide to the characters and the context. (See sample texts.)

2 Make enough copies for the whole class.

IN CLASS

1 Give the students copies of the passage. Ask them to read it through and note down their suggestions for the missing words.

2 After five to eight minutes, ask them to form groups of four and compare notes. During the discussion they should note down any fresh ideas which emerge.

3 *Class discussion*. Ask each group to call out its suggestions. Write up as many as you can on the board, or ask two students to help with the writing.

4 Go over the students' suggestions, and ask them to help you correct any errors or awkward formulations. Then reveal the original wording.

NOTES

1 The emphasis in this activity is on the spoken language. It is important, therefore, in selecting the material to look for passages of dialogue which are close to everyday speech, and which will draw suggestions from the students without demanding great ingenuity.

2 You will find, in preparing the material, that there are many ways of giving a particular language focus to the activity. For instance, in text 1, you could concentrate on the use of contracted forms such as *I've, I'll, You'll, You're*, by leaving blank the remarks in which these forms occur.

In the discussion, encourage the students to offer as many suggestions as possible, for in this activity many different wordings can be correct. For example:

'*Your taxi's* just left/already gone/driving away/not waiting/off' are all equally valid.

3 If your students have set books to study, they may find this an enjoyable way of reviving tired texts.

4 See also activity 4.1 *Focus on language*.

SAMPLE TEXTS

1 Summary

The narrator ('I') is employed at the American Embassy in London. Recently, he has met Sophie Graveney, an attractive, but somewhat distant woman 'in the full bloom of thirty'. In this scene they are going home after their first dinner together.

I paid for the taxi, then walked with her to the front gate.
She said, 'Your taxi's (1) . . . .'
'I've paid him. I told him to go.'
'(2) . . . . You'll never get another one around here – and the buses (3) . . . .'
I said, 'Then I'll walk,' and clung to her hand, 'although (4) . . . .'
'It's not far to your hotel.'
'I didn't mean that. I just meant I'd rather (5) . . . .'
'I know,' she said. 'You're sweet.'
The English are frugal. They can even economize on words. Sophie gave nothing away. She planted a rather perfunctory kiss on my cheek, and when I tried to embrace her she eased out of my grasp and said comically, '(6) . . .', and took out her door-key.
'You're beautiful,' I said.
'I'm tired,' she said. 'I must (7) . . . .'
I said, 'I want to see you again soon.'
'(8) . . .,' she said.

(Paul Theroux: *The London Embassy*)

2 Summary

Sarah and Louise are sisters. Louise has made a 'brilliant marriage', and no longer needs to work. Sarah, however, needs a job, and is thinking of leaving home to look for work in London. She receives a letter from her friend, Gill, suggesting that they look for a flat together. In the extract below, Sarah (me) broaches the subject to her mother. The conversation went along these well-oiled grooves:

Me   Mummy, I've been thinking, I think (1) . . . to London at the end of the week.
Mama (pause) Oh yes?
Me   Yes, a friend of mine wants someone to share a flat and I thought it would be (2) . . . for me to . . .
Mama Well, that sounds a very good idea. Where exactly is this flat?
Me   Well, we haven't exactly got one, but I thought I might (3) . . . – it's easier if you're on the spot.
Mama Oh yes, I'm sure it is. I hear it's very difficult to find flats in London these days.
Me   (my heart sinking as I think of adverts, agencies, *Evening Standards*, et cetera) Oh no, it's not at all difficult, people get themselves fixed up in no time.
Mama Oh well, I suppose you (4) . . . than me. What will you (5) . . . while you're there?
Me   I'll get a job. I'll have to sometime, you know.
Mama Just any sort of job?

Me   Whatever there is.

Mama   Don't you want a proper *career*, Sarah?

Me   No, not really. I don't know what I want to do.

Mama   I'm not sure I like the idea of your going off all the way to
           London without a proper job and with nowhere to live . . .
           still, it's your own life, I suppose. No one can accuse me of
           trying to keep you at home, either of you . . . Who is this
           friend of yours?

Me   A girl called Gill Slater.

Mama   And what (6) . . .?

Me   Oh, she's a – she's a sort of research student.

Mama   (7) . . .? Well, it sounds like a very nice idea. After all, you
           won't want to stay here all your life cooped up with your poor
           old mother, will you? I shall lose all my little ones at one fell
           swoop, shall I?

Me   Oh don't be silly.

Mama   What do you mean, don't be silly? It seems to me you're very
           eager to be off.

Me   You know that's not it at all.

Mama   Well, what is it then?

Me   Well, it's just that I can't (8) . . ., can I?

Mama   No, of course you can't, nobody ever suggested anything of
           the sort. When have I ever tried to keep you at home? Haven't
           I just said that you must lead your own life? And you can't say
           that staying at home for a week just after you've got back from
           abroad is (9) . . ., can you? I've hardly had a chance to see you
           yet, and you're off. I sometimes wonder what you and Louise
           bother to come home for. You just use home as if (10) . . .,
           you two. All I am is a servant, that's all I am . . .

Me   Don't say that, don't say that, of course I'll stay, it (11) . . . at
           all.

Mama   (in floods of tears) Oh, I know there's nothing to keep you
           here, I know there's no reason why you (12) . . ., there's
           nothing to amuse you, you've outgrown it all, you always were
           too clever for me.

Me   (weeping too) Oh don't, please don't, Mummy, please don't,
           I'll stay with you as long as you like, you know I will.

Mama   (sniffing and reasserting her hairpins) No, don't be silly. Of
           course you (13) . . ., what on earth would you do with yourself
           here. You go off to London, you'll be (14) . . . there.

Me   No, I don't want to go any more.

Mama   Oh yes, you really ought to go. So let's have (15) . . ., shall
           we?
           (And so I went to London at the end of the week.)

           (Margaret Drabble: *A Summer Bird-Cage*)

3 Summary

Betty announces to her friend , Carruthers, that she has suddenly decided to get married. She asks him if he would join her for a drink at Claridge's before she has to go on to the family meeting.

'He's bringing his family to luncheon today to meet father. I dare say it'll be (1) . . . You might stand me a cocktail at Claridge's to fortify me, will you?'

'At what time?' he asked.

'One.'

'All right. I'll meet you there.'

He was waiting for her when she came in. She walked with a sort of spring as though her eager feet itched to break into a dance. She was smiling. Carruthers really felt that she brought sunshine and the scent of flowers into the sober but rather overwhelming splendour of Claridge's lounge. He did not wait to say (2) . . . to her.

'Betty, you (3) . . ,' he said. 'It's simply out of the question.'

'Why?'

'He's awful.'

'(4) . . . I think he's rather nice.'

Betty looked at Carruthers with those beautiful eyes of hers that managed to be at the same time so gay and so tender.

'He's such a frightful bounder, Betty.'

'Oh, don't be so silly, Humphrey. He's (5) . . . I think you're rather a snob.'

'He's so dull'.

'No, he's (6) . . . I don't know that I want a husband who's too brilliant. I think he'll (7) . . . He's quite good-looking and he has nice manners.'

'My God, Betty. Are you going to pretend you're in love with him?'

'I think (8) . . ., don't you?'

'Why are you (9) . . .?'

'He's got pots of money. I'm (10) . . .'

There was nothing much more to be said. He drove her back to her aunt's house. She had a very grand marriage.

(Somerset Maugham: *The Human Element*)

KEY

Original wording:

Text 1: Paul Theroux: *The London Embassy*

1 driving away
2 That was silly.
3 have stopped running.
4 I don't want to.
5 stay here with you.
6 Do you *mind?*
7 get some sleep.
8 I'd like that.

Text 2: Margaret Drabble: *A Summer Bird-Cage*

1   I might go
2   a good opportunity
3   go and look
4   know better
5   live on
6   does she do?
7   Oh yes?
8   stay here all my life
9   stay at home *all your life*
10 it were a hotel
11 doesn't matter to me
12 should stay here
13 can't stay here
14 better off
15 no more nonsense

Text 3: Somerset Maugham: *The Human Element*

1   a bit grim.
2   how do you do
3   can't do it
4   I don't think he is.
5   just as good as anybody else.
6   rather quiet.
7   make a very good background.
8   it would be tactful
9   going to marry him?
10 nearly twenty-six.

2.8 Completing the picture

LEVEL

Advanced

TIME

30 – 45 minutes

PREPARATION

1 Select a passage of between twelve and twenty pages from a novel. Look in particular for passages in which the reader learns something new or unexpected.

2 Read through the passage you have chosen, then select four or five pages of the text on which you wish the students to concentrate.

3 Divide the pages you have chosen into four or five roughly equal sections.

If you feel that the students will not be able to understand the situation out of context, prepare a brief explanation, or use one section of the text as an introduction. (The texts used in this activity are a continuation of the incident described in 2.4 *Storylines 2: suspense*. The students will, therefore, already be familiar with *The Woman in White*. We have, however, also added an introduction, taken from the text of the novel, as an aid to comprehension.)

4 Prepare copies of the sections you have chosen (as in sample texts B). Each group of three students will need a copy of only one of the sections. Also prepare copies of the introduction (sample text A) for the whole class.

IN CLASS

1 Give the class a brief outline of the story of the novel up to the point you have chosen. Explain who the characters are, and where they are. Then distribute the introduction for silent reading.

2 Ask the students to form groups of three. Give each group a copy of one of the sections you have prepared. Ask them to read through their texts and to note down any questions they would like to ask of the other groups (who have different sections).

3 After about ten minutes, ask each group to join with any other group which has been working on a different section. Together, they exchange questions and, where possible, answers. (If time permits, ask the students to change groups once again.)

4 *Class discussion*. The students call out any questions that are still unresolved. Other members of the class offer answers.

5 (Optional) *Listening*. Play a recording of the text.

NOTES

1 In planning this activity, you may find it helpful to think in visual terms. That is, to imagine that the sequence you have chosen from the novel is being shown on television, and that the students' viewing has been interrupted at some stage, say, by a telephone call. Each student will want to know what happened before or after the interruption. The aim of the discussion, then, is to find out what happens and to piece together the missing bits.

2 Clearly, an activity such as this will work best with an unfamiliar text. If the story is already known, part of the interest is lost. But the technique can also be used with familiar works of fiction, such as *Oliver Twist*, *Madame Bovary*, or *Anna Karenina*. In such cases, you could try a slightly different approach. Instead of giving the students consecutive passages (that is, four or five pages in sequence), you could present them with short passages from different parts of the text and ask them to fill in the missing narrative.

3 See also 2.4 *Storylines 2: suspense*, and the listening activities in Section 4.

SAMPLE TEXT A

Introduction

(After meeting the woman in white, the narrator, Mr Hartright, travels on to Limmeridge House, where he meets his two art students, Miss Halcombe and Miss Fairlie. Here, he is talking to Miss Halcombe. He has not yet met Miss Fairlie.)

'The very night before I arrived at this house, I met with an adventure; and the wonder and excitement of it, I can assure you, Miss Halcombe, will last me for the whole term of my stay in Cumberland, if not for a much longer period.'

'You don't say so, Mr Hartright! May I hear it?'

'You have a claim to hear it. The chief person in the adventure was a total stranger to me, and may perhaps be a total stranger to you; but she certainly mentioned the name of the late Mrs Fairlie in terms of the sincerest gratitude and regard.'

'Mentioned my mother's name! You interest me indescribably. Pray go on.'

I at once related the circumstances under which I had met the woman in white, exactly as they had occurred; and I repeated what she had said to me about Mrs Fairlie and Limmeridge House, word for word.

Miss Halcombe's bright resolute eyes looked eagerly into mine, from the beginning of the narrative to the end. Her face expressed vivid interest and astonishment, but nothing more. She was evidently as far from knowing of any clue to the mystery as I was myself.

'Are you quite sure of those words referring to my mother?' she asked.

'Quite sure,' I replied. 'Whoever she may be, the woman was at school in the village of Limmeridge, was treated with especial kindness by Mrs Fairlie, and, in grateful remembrance of that kindness, feels an affectionate interest in all surviving members of the family. She knew that Mrs Fairlie and her husband were both dead; and she spoke of Miss Fairlie as if they had known each other when they were children.'

'You said, I think, that she denied belonging to this place?'

'Yes, she told me she came from Hampshire.'

'And you entirely failed to find out her name?'

'Entirely.'

'Very strange. I think you were quite justified, Mr Hartright, in giving the poor creature her liberty, for she seems to have done nothing in your presence to show herself unfit to enjoy it. But I wish you had been a little more resolute about finding out her name. We must really clear up this mystery, in some way. You had better not speak of it yet to Mr Fairlie, or to my sister. They are both of them, I am certain, quite as ignorant of who the woman is, and of what her past history in connection with us can be, as I am myself. But they are also, in widely different ways, rather nervous and sensitive . . . As for myself, I am all aflame with curiosity, and I devote my whole energies to the business of discovery from this moment. When my mother came here, after her second marriage, she certainly established the village school just as it exists at the present time.

My sister and I have a large collection of my mother's letters, addressed to my father and to hers. In the absence of any other means of getting information, I will pass the morning in looking over my mother's correspondence with Mr Fairlie. He was fond of London, and was constantly away from his country home; and she was accustomed, at such times, to write and report to him on how things went on at Limmeridge. Her letters are full of references to the school in which she took so strong an interest; and I think it more than likely that I may have discovered something when we meet again.'

SAMPLE TEXTS B   1 We had been out on the terrace together, just in front of the glass doors, hardly so long as five minutes, I should think; and Miss Fairlie was, by my advice, just tying her white handkerchief over her head as a precaution against the night air – when I heard Miss Halcombe's voice – low, eager, and altered from its natural lively tone – pronounce my name.

'Mr Hartright,' she said, 'will you come here for a minute? I want to speak to you.'

I entered the room again immediately. The piano stood about halfway down along the inner wall. On the side of the instrument farthest from the terrace Miss Halcombe was sitting with the letters scattered on her lap, and with one in her hand selected from them, and held close to the candle. On the side nearest to the terrace there stood a low couch, on which I took my place. In this position I was not far from the glass doors, and I could see Miss Fairlie plainly, as she passed and repassed the opening on to the terrace, walking slowly from end to end of it in the full radiance of the moon.

'I want you to listen while I read the concluding passages in this letter,' said Miss Halcombe. 'Tell me if you think they throw any light upon your strange adventure on the road to London. The letter is addressed by my mother to her second husband, Mr Fairlie, and the date refers to a period of between eleven and twelve years ago. At that time Mr and Mrs Fairlie, and my half-sister Laura, had been living for years in this house; and I was away from them completing my education at a school in Paris.'

She looked and spoke earnestly, and, as I thought, a little uneasily as well. At the moment when she raised the letter to the candle before beginning to read it, Miss Fairlie passed us on the terrace, looked in for a moment, and seeing that we were engaged, slowly walked on.

--✂

2 Miss Halcombe began to read as follows:

' "You will be tired, my dear Philip, of hearing perpetually about my school and my scholars. Lay the blame, pray, on the dull uniformity of life at Limmeridge, and not on me. Besides, this time I have something really interesting to tell you about a new scholar.

' "You know old Mrs Kempe at the village shop. Well, after years of ailing, the doctor has at last given her up, and she is dying slowly day by day. Her only living relation, a sister, arrived last week to take care of her. This sister comes all the way from Hampshire – her name is Mrs Catherick. Four days ago Mrs Catherick came here to see me, and brought her only child with her, a sweet little girl about a year older than our darling Laura –" '

As the last sentence fell from the reader's lips, Miss Fairlie passed us on the terrace once more. She was softly singing to herself one of the melodies which she had been playing earlier in the evening. Miss Halcombe waited till she had passed out of sight again, and then went on with the letter –

" 'Mrs Catherick is a decent, well-behaved, respectable woman; middle-aged, and with the remains of having been moderately, only moderately, nice-looking. There is something in her manner and in her appearance, however, I can't make out. She is reserved about herself, and there is a look on her face – I can't describe it – which suggests to me that she has something on her mind. She is altogether what you would call a walking mystery. Her errand at Limmeridge House, however, was simple enough. When she left Hampshire to nurse her sister, Mrs Kempe, through her last illness, she had been obliged to bring her daughter with her, through having no one at home to take care of the little girl. Mrs Kempe may die in a week's time, or may linger on for months; and Mrs Catherick's object was to ask me to let her daughter, Anne, have the benefit of attending my school, subject to the condition of her being removed from it to go home again with her mother, after Mrs Kempe's death. I consented at once, and when Laura and I went out for our walk, we took the little girl (who is just eleven years old) to the school that very day." '

--✂

3 Once more Miss Fairlie's figure, bright and soft in its snowy muslin dress – her face prettily framed by the white folds of the handkerchief which she had tied under her chin – passed by us in the moonlight. Once more Miss Halcombe waited till she was out of sight, and then went on –

' "I have taken a violent fancy, Philip, to my new scholar, for a reason which I mean to keep till the last for the sake of surprising you. Her mother having told me as little about the child as she told me of herself, I was left to discover (which I did on the first day when we tried her at lessons) that the poor little thing's intellect is not developed as it ought to be at her age. Seeing this I had her up to the house the next day, and privately arranged with the doctor to come and watch her and question her, and tell me what he thought. His opinion is that she will grow out of it. But he says her careful bringing-up at school is a matter of great importance just now, because her unusual slowness in acquiring ideas implies an unusual tenacity in keeping them, when they are once received into her mind. Now, my love, you must not imagine, in your off-hand way, that I have been attaching myself to an idiot. This poor little Anne Catherick is a sweet, affectionate, grateful girl, and says the quaintest, prettiest things, in the most oddly sudden, surprised, half-frightened way. Although she is dressed very neatly, her clothes show a sad want of taste in colour and pattern. So I arranged, yesterday, that some of our darling Laura's old white frocks and white hats should be altered for Anne Catherick, explaining to her that little girls of her complexion looked neater and better all in white than in anything else. She hesitated and seemed puzzled for a minute, then flushed up, and appeared to understand. Her little hand clasped mine suddenly. She kissed it, Philip, and said (oh, so earnestly!), 'I will always wear white as long as I live. It will help me to remember you, ma'am, and to think that I am pleasing you still, when I go away and see you no more.' This is only one specimen of the quaint things she says so prettily. Poor little soul! She shall have a stock of white frocks, made with good deep tucks, to let out for her as she grows –" '

Miss Halcombe paused, and looked at me across the piano.

'Did the forlorn woman whom you met in the high-road seem young?' she asked. 'Young enough to be two- or three-and-twenty?'

'Yes, Miss Halcombe, as young as that.'

'And she was strangely dressed, from head to foot, all in white?'

'All in white.'

---✁

4 While the answer was passing my lips Miss Fairlie glided into view on the terrace for the third time. Instead of proceeding on her walk, she stopped, with her back turned towards us, and, leaning on the balustrade of the terrace, looked down into the garden beyond. My eyes fixed upon the white gleam of her muslin gown and head-dress in the moonlight, and a sensation, for which I can find no name – a sensation that quickened my pulse, and raised a fluttering at my heart – began to steal over me.

'All in white?' Miss Halcombe repeated. 'The most important sentences in the letter, Mr Hartright, are those at the end, which I will read to you immediately. But I can't help dwelling a little upon the coincidence of the white costume of the woman you met, and the white frocks which produced that strange answer from my mother's little scholar. The doctor may have been wrong when he discovered the child's defects of intellect, and predicted that she would 'grow out of them.' She may never have grown out of them, and the old fancy about dressing in white, which was a serious feeling to the girl, may be a serious feeling to the woman still.'

I said a few words in answer – I hardly know what. All my attention was concentrated on the white gleam of Miss Fairlie's muslin dress.

'Listen to the last sentences of the letter,' said Miss Halcombe. 'I think they will surprise you.'

As she raised the letter to the light of the candle, Miss Fairlie turned from the balustrade, looked doubtfully up and down the terrace, advanced a step towards the glass doors, and then stopped, facing us.

Meanwhile Miss Halcombe read me the last sentences to which she had referred.

--✂

5 ' "And now, my love, seeing that I am at the end of my paper, now for the little reason, the surprising reason, for my fondness for little Anne Catherick. My dear Philip, although she is not half so pretty, she is, nevertheless, by one of those extraordinary caprices of accidental resemblance which one sometimes sees, the living likeness, in her hair, her complexion, the colour of her eyes, and the shape of her face–" '

I started up from the couch before Miss Halcombe could pronounce the next words. A thrill of the same feeling which ran through me when the touch was laid upon my shoulder on the lonely high-road chilled me again.

There stood Miss Fairlie, a white figure, alone in the moonlight; in her attitude, in the turn of her head, in her complexion, in the shape of her face, the living image, at that distance and under those circumstances, of the woman in white! The doubt which had troubled my mind for hours and hours past flashed into conviction in an instant. That 'something wanting' was my own recognition of the ominous likeness between the fugitive from the asylum and my pupil at Limmeridge House.

'You see it!' said Miss Halcombe. She dropped the useless letter, and her eyes flashed as they met mine. 'You see it now, as my mother saw it eleven years since!'

'I see it – more unwillingly than I can say. To associate that forlorn, friendless, lost woman, even by an accidental likeness only, with Miss Fairlie, seems like casting a shadow on the future of the bright creature who stands looking at us now. Let me lose the impression again as soon as possible. Call her in, out of the dreary moonlight – pray call her in!'

'Mr Hartright, you surprise me. Whatever women may be, I thought that men, in the nineteenth century, were above superstition.'

'Pray call her in!'

'Hush, hush! She is coming of her own accord. Say nothing in her presence. Let this discovery of the likeness be kept a secret between you and me. Come in, Laura, come in, and wake Mrs Vesey with the piano.

So ended my eventful first day at Limmeridge House.

3 Developing ideas: themes, topics, and projects

Introduction

> I am a camera with its shutter open, quite passive, recording not
> thinking. Recording the man shaving at the window opposite and
> the woman in the kimono washing her hair. Some day all of this
> will have to be developed, carefully printed, fixed.
>
> (Christopher Isherwood)

Personal experience is the theme running through this section.
Memories, recollections, chance thoughts, observations, personal
reactions – all of these will be drawn upon in the activities.

Like Christopher Isherwood, each student can say: 'I am a camera
with its shutter open.' And each has different pictures to offer. We
believe that they are worth 'developing'.

In the main *Introduction*, we mentioned some of the drawbacks to
the conventional question-and-answer approach to literature. Of
these, two of the most serious are:
1 The students are restricted by the nature of the questions.
Discussion is confined to those parts of the text on which questions
are asked, and these are not necessarily the parts which interest the
student.
2 The text itself is made the sole focus of attention and little
opportunity is given for developing the ideas suggested by the text.

One way of overcoming these drawbacks is to alter our approach to
the text. Instead of making it the focal point of the activity, we
allow it to become instead a point of reference. This can be done,
for instance, by first allowing the students to discuss a topic related
to the text. This will be a free discussion, not influenced by
anything the students have read. Next, the text can be introduced
as material to spark off further ideas. Finally, the students can be
asked to take their discussion a stage further, sharing any fresh
ideas suggested by the text(s).

In *Developing ideas*, we have tried to strike a proper balance
between the two extremes of rigidity and looseness. The discussion
is not bound solely to the text, but it is also not completely open-
ended. The texts suggest the themes; the students develop them.

About the activities

The activities fall into two groups:

In the first group (3.1 *Picture stories*, 3.2 *Creating situations from dialogue*, 3.3 *Screen adaptation*), the emphasis is on creation and transformation. In *Picture stories*, the students begin by creating their own stories from a set of pictures which they arrange in sequence as illustrations of key points in their story. Next, they work – almost in reverse – on a sequence of pictures on the events in a short story. Their task is to recreate the story in their own words. Here, the text itself comes right at the end of the activity. By contrast, in *Creating situations from dialogue* and *Screen adaptation*, the texts serve as the starting point for two kinds of transformation.

In the second group (3.4 – 3.8 *Discussion topics*), the emphasis is on the students' personal involvement with a given theme or topic. Two important features which these five activities have in common are:

1 They involve the use of several texts, including in some cases non-fictional writing. Although one of the passages may be chosen to introduce the topic (the poem 'Cathedral Builders' in 3.4 *Difficult jobs*, for instance), this does not mean that it needs to remain the focus of later discussions.

2 All the activities are designed to touch on areas of experience about which the students can, if they wish, speak freely from personal knowledge. Even if they themselves have never done any difficult jobs (see activity 3.4), they will have observed others (perhaps their own parents) at work; and there can be no student who does not have childhood memories (see activity 3.6).

What we are proposing in this section is that literature should not be divorced from life, and also that students should be encouraged to see the link between their own worlds and the no less real world of literature.

3.1 Picture stories

LEVEL

Lower intermediate to advanced

TIME

40 minutes (2 × 20 minutes)

PREPARATION

There are two stages to this activity. For each stage you will need different materials.

Stage one

Prepare a class set of about thirty pictures of *people*, *objects*, and *places*. There should be enough pictures to allow you to distribute at least five to each group.

Stage two

1 Prepare a set of simple line drawings illustrating certain key points in a story you have chosen. An example is given on page 90. If you are not good at drawing, ask the students to help. (See the comments in *Notes*.)

2 Make enough copies for the whole class, or prepare a transparency for display on the OHP.

IN CLASS

Stage one

1 Ask the students to form groups of three. Give each group a set of five or six pictures of people, objects, and places.

2 Tell each group to invent a story based on the pictures. All the pictures must be used, but the students may add anything that is needed to complete the story (for example, an aeroplane, or a customs officer).

3 When ready, each group lays out its pictures in the order in which they occur in their story. Any important additional details can be written on slips of paper and placed between the pictures, like this:

Picture 1	Picture 2	Picture 3	Picture 4	Picture 5	Picture 6
	aeroplane/ taxi	customs officer		casino	

4 Ask one student in each group to stay with the pictures. The rest now move around to other groups and try to work out the stories by looking at the pictures. The student who stays with the pictures should listen to the suggestions and give hints, before finally revealing the story.

Stage two

1 Hand out photocopies of the line drawings for the story, or display them on the OHP. Ask the class to suggest what happens in the story.

2 After listening to the students' suggestions, read out fragments of the text relating to each picture. After each short passage, allow time for the students to revise their earlier suggestions.

3 *Listening.* If possible, let the students listen to a recording of the whole story. If not, try to make copies of it available for out-of-class reading.

NOTES

1 A story can be sparked off by very small details – a smell, a gesture, a sudden sound, or a chance remark. (Somerset Maugham, for instance, said that his short story 'Rain' developed out of a few brief notes in his diary.) The purpose of the introductory activity (*Stage one*) is to put the students in the right frame of mind for speculation, by inviting them to devise their own stories from a few visual pointers. The pictures suggest a framework which they can fill in as they like.

2 In *Stage two*, the activity becomes more controlled. The students are not inventing, but re-creating a story from pictures. But they do not have the text. The challenge, then, is to build up a plausible story in their own words.

3 *Stage two* of the activity may be difficult to prepare, particularly if you feel you are not good at drawing. If so, why not enlist the help of the students? Give them the key words (*snake, bed, doctor's bag*) and ask them to draw the pictures.

4 Other books which may be helpful in developing this activity are: Wright: *Visual Materials for the Language Teacher*; Maley, Duff, and Grellet: *The Mind's Eye*; and Hedge: *Writing* and Greenwood: *Class Readers*, both in this series.

SOURCE

The line drawings on page 90 are picture cues designed to be used with Roald Dahl's short story: 'Poison'. If you wish to work with these drawings and Roald Dahl's text, try to obtain a copy of the story to read to the class at the end of the activity.

3.2 Creating situations from dialogue

LEVEL   Intermediate

TIME   30 minutes

PREPARATION   For this activity you will need short passages of dialogue which are easy to speak, and which are also open to interpretation. Suitable extracts can easily be found in the works of modern playwrights such as Beckett, Pinter, Pirandello, Ionesco, and others.

1 Copy out the dialogue as shown in the sample texts. Replace the characters' names with letters (A, B, or C), and leave out any stage directions.

2 Make enough copies for one third of the class.

IN CLASS   1 Ask the students to form groups of three. Give each group a copy of one of the texts you have chosen, or, if you prefer, give each group the same text.

2 Set a time-limit (twelve to fifteen minutes). Ask the students to expand the text by writing dialogue of their own to come before and after the passage (about six lines in each case).

Tell the students to imagine that the dialogue is part of a play. They should therefore decide on their own answers to the following questions:

– *Who are the characters (A and B)?*
– *Where are they, and why are they there?*
– *What is happening, and going to happen?*
– *Is there a third person present?*

3 When the students are ready, ask each group to perform its version of the dialogue for another group. In turn, the observing groups try to work out what was happening in the performance. (The performers should not immediately give an explanation, but instead respond to the observers' questions.) Allow time for each group to see at least two different performances.

NOTES   1 It is important that the material you choose should be easy to speak. Students are often asked to speak lines which they cannot get their tongues around. This leads to embarrassment, which is one of the reasons why 'performances' in a foreign language often fall flat.

In this activity, the stress should not be on performance but on interpretation. If any of the students would prefer not to act out their dialogue, but rather read it sitting down, let them do so. There will still be plenty to discuss.

2 For a similar activity using dialogue drawn from novels and short stories, see 1.7 *Speculation 1*.

SOURCES

Passages 1 and 2: Harold Pinter: *Silence*
Passage 3: Brian Friel: *Translations*
Passage 4: H. E. Bates: *Fair Stood the Wind for France*

SAMPLE TEXTS

1 **A** Will we meet tonight?
  B I don't know.
  A Come with me tonight.
  B Where?
  A Anywhere. For a walk.
  B I don't want to walk.
  A What do you want to do?
  B I don't know.
  A Come for a walk.
  B No.
  A I walk in my mind. But can't get out of the walls, into a wind.
    Meadows are walled, and lakes. The sky's a wall.

2 **A** Do you like music?
  B Yes.
  A I'll play you music.
  B It's very dark outside.
  A It's high up.
  B Does it get darker the higher you get?
  A No.
  B Around me sits the night. Such a silence. I can hear myself.
    Cup my ear. My heart beats in my ear. Such a silence. Is it
    me? Am I silent or speaking? How can I know?

3 **A** May I come? Would anyone object if I came?
  B What's he saying?
  C Who would object?
  B Did you tell him?
  A Sorry-sorry?
  C He says may he come?
  B That's up to you.
  A What does she say?
  C She says –
  A What-what?
  B Well?
  A Sorry-sorry?
  C Will you go?
  A Yes, yes, if I may.

4 **A** Would you be ready to do something?
  B For you?
  A For yourself. Would you be ready to go?
  B When?
  A Tonight. The man who came here is no good. He was here for
    no good. We know him. He has an idea of something, and if
    he has an idea he will talk about it.

3.3 Screen adaptation

LEVEL **Intermediate to advanced**

TIME **30 – 45 minutes**

PREPARATION **1** Select a passage from a novel or short story which you think would be suitable for adapting for the screen (film or TV).

2 Make enough copies for the whole class.

3 Give the students the whole text to read at home. Ask them to think over how they would adapt it for the screen. In particular, they should mark any parts of the text which they think would be difficult to convey in a film, such as the following examples from the sample text:

– *He must be a wizard at interrogation!*
– *. . . it added to the sense I had of the coldness of the occasion.*
– *You know how people talk about faces 'closing up'? I think 'close down' is nearer to it . . . What actually happens is that the face remains exactly the same but all the lights go out.*

IN CLASS **1** *Class discussion.* Ask the class to call out any parts of the text which they think would be difficult or even impossible to show on the screen. Note these, briefly, on the blackboard.

2 Ask the students to form groups of three. Give each group a number: 1, 2, 3, or 4 (there may be several groups with each number). The numbers correspond to the four sections into which the text is divided. They work like this: group(s) 1 on section 1, group(s) 2 on section 2, and so on.

3 Write up on the blackboard the following outline for a camera script:

Camera script
a. *What the text says:*
He was often pretty lonely. He knew he hadn't much to offer.

b. *What the camera shows:*
The camera is behind Merrick's back, looking over his shoulder. It shows Daphne's face as she listens to him.

c. *What words are spoken:*
'I feel pretty lonely at times. I know I haven't much to offer.'

Ask each group to draw up a camera script for their sequence. They should describe the sequence in not more than three different shots. Each shot should be described in the same way:

– *What the text says*
– *What the camera shows*
– *What words are spoken.*

4 Each group then joins another which has worked on the same sequence from the text (each group 1 joins another group 1, groups 2 join up, and so on). Together, they compare their different versions of the text.

5 If time permits, the groups can also go on to discuss their camera scripts with those who have worked on different sequences.

1 As a language activity, this exercise in visualization has several advantages:

a. It allows the students to come to grips with a text without having to answer specific questions about it. They, in fact, will be asking their own questions (for instance, is Daphne attracted to Merrick, or does she simply feel sorry for him?).

b. It is an activity which naturally generates discussion, because the text is open to interpretation. (When Daphne says 'Perhaps I ought to have taken my specs out', does she make a movement on screen or not?)

c. The students are free to adapt the language, for instance by turning reported speech into direct speech: His other regret was that he'd never 'met the right sort of girl for him'.

2 Teachers (and, more rarely, students) occasionally object that they know nothing about film technique. In fact, to do this activity you do not need to know anything about filming or film technique. You need only to have watched a few films. The camera script does not need to look like a professional document. It simply helps to give a clear focus to the activity.

3 This activity can be made even more interesting if the students have an opportunity to see a screen adaptation of a novel or short story. Try contacting your local television station to find out what English films they plan to show during the year. You could use the original works as material for this activity. The students would then have the satisfaction of seeing how the director solved the problems they too had faced.

SAMPLE TEXT

The MacGregor House
MacGregor Road
Mayapore 1

Friday, 17th July 1942

Dear Auntie Ethel,

1   Many thanks for your letter and news of the goings on in
Srinagar. Glad you got the photograph safely and in time for your
birthday, but gladder still that you like the dress length. The
photograph seemed to me so awful that I had to send something else
as well to make up for it, and then wondered choosing that colour
whether I hadn't made everything worse! ...

     ... I mostly get a lift to and from the hospital in Mr Mer-
rick's car which he sends round with a police driver. I find it a
bit embarrassing and have told him several times that I can quite
easily go on my bicycle on <u>any</u> day, but he insists it's really his
duty to see I don't come to any harm.

     I like him better than I used to. I can't close my eyes to
the fact that he's been kind and considerate. It's his manner
that's against him (and something behind his manner, naturally).
And of course a District Superintendent of Police <u>is</u> a bit off-
putting. But now that I've got used to him - and got over something that I think I must tell you - I quite enjoy the times he
takes me out ...

     ... I feel I must tell you, <u>but please keep it to yourself</u>.
About a month ago he invited me to his bungalow for dinner. He'd
gone to a lot of trouble. It was the best English meal I've had in
India ...

2   ... (After dinner) while we were drinking he asked me a lot
of questions about my family, about how David was killed, and
about Daddy, and then about me, and what I thought about life and
all that sort of thing, but in a chatty, sympathetic way that made
me open up. (He must be a wizard at interrogation! That's not
fair. But you know what I mean.) Gradually I realized he had begun
to talk about himself. And I was thinking: People don't like you
much, but you're fundamentally <u>kind,</u> and that's why you and I
have always got on surprisingly well.

... He said he came of 'a very ordinary family', and his
grandparents had been 'pretty humble sort of people'. He had
worked hard and done all right so far in the Indian Police, and
his main regret was that being in it he wasn't allowed to join up.
His other regret was that he'd never really had any 'youth', or
'met the right sort of girl for him'. He was often 'pretty
lonely'. He knew he hadn't much to offer. He realized his background and mine were 'rather different'. Our friendship meant a
lot to him.

Then he dried up. I just didn't know what to say, because I
didn't know if I'd understood or misunderstood what he was driving
at. We sort of stared at each other for a while. Then he said,
'I'm only asking whether after you've had time to think about it
you'd consider the possibility of becoming engaged to me.'

3   Do you know, Auntie, that's the only proposal I've ever had?
I'm sure by the time you were my age you'd had dozens. Does every
girl find the first one oddly moving? I suppose it depends on the
man. But if he's, you know, all right, decent enough, you can't
not be touched, can you, whatever you feel about him as a person?
I don't think my feelings for Ronald Merrick could ever be described as more than passingly affectionate ... I never feel quite
natural when I'm with him, but can never be sure whether that is
my fault or his. But when he came out with this request (you can
hardly call it a proposal, can you?) I wanted very much to have
been able to make things all right for him and say 'Yes' ...

What made it so extraordinary was that he never so much as
touched my hand. At the time, this not touching added to my wish
not to hurt him. Later, thinking about, it added to the sense I
had of the coldness surrounding the occasion. We were sitting at
opposite ends of the sofa. Perhaps I ought to have taken my specs
out and put them on! Looking back on it I can't really recall
whether I felt that what had been said was a shock or not. It
seemed to be a shock, but in retrospect the whole evening was
obviously leading up to it, so I can't think why I should have
been surprised, or even believe that I was.

4   There must have been lots of things said before he came out
with it that I inwardly took notice of. At some stage or other I
decided that physically, in spite of his looks, he repelled me,
but I think that came later, and was only momentary ... The faint

feeling of repulsion probably came through because of the sense I had of relief, of having got out of a difficult situation and retreated <u>into myself</u> in a way that left no room for others who-ever they might be.

I was now more concerned about the possible effect of my 'refusal'. Honestly, I'm sure that all I said was 'thank you, Ronald - but -' but that was enough. You know how people talk about faces 'closing up'? I think 'close down' is nearer to it, because 'close up' suggests a sort of <u>constriction</u>, a <u>change</u>, whereas what actually happens is that the face remains exactly the same but all the lights go out. Like a house where people have gone away. If you knock at the door now there won't be any answer.

... Presently he drove me home and we talked quite easily about nothing. He escorted me up the steps to the verandah. When we shook hands he hung on to mine for a moment and said, 'Some ideas take getting used to,' from which I gathered he hadn't yet given up, but it was a different man who said it. The District Superintendent of Police, the Ronald Merrick I don't care for.

(Paul Scott: *The Jewel in the Crown*)

3.4 Discussion topics 1: difficult jobs

LEVEL   Advanced

TIME   30 – 45 minutes

PREPARATION   1 Choose a poem or a prose passage which suggests a topic that might be developed in class discussion. Look for two or three other texts (fictional or non-fictional) which are related to the topic.

2 Prepare sufficient copies of the texts for each group of |three students to have one set. (See sample texts for a selection of literature relating to the activity described below.)

3 Also, collect any visual material you can find which is related to the topic, such as a large poster showing a European medieval cathedral, or any other architectural wonder.

IN CLASS   1 *Preliminary discussion*. Write up on the board the words *Old Buildings*. Ask the class to name any famous ancient monuments in their own country or elsewhere in the world, for instance the Egyptian pyramids, the Forbidden City in Beijing, the Tower of London, and so on.

2 Then ask the students to think of some of the difficulties that the ancient architects and building workers had to face. Note these on the board:

– *They had to clear forests, drain swamps, build on sand*
– *They had no drilling equipment, dynamite, cement, plastic covers, tarred roads for transport of material*
– *The climate was very hot/cold/wet*
– *They had little or no job security; they had to move from one job to another, even from one country to another, and had little family life*
– *The work was dangerous.*

3 If possible, show the class a picture of a medieval cathedral, a mosque, a temple, a pyramid, a Khmer monument, or an Inca palace, and ask them to say which parts of each building must have been the most difficult to construct and why. Make a note of their suggestions.

4 Ask the students to form groups of three. Give them copies of the extract from 'The long climb back to glory'. They should read the text and note any details which have been mentioned in the earlier discussion, for example:
– *the work was dangerous* ('You pass graffiti commemorating a mason who fell in the 16th century'.)

5 Now, write up on the blackboard or display on the OHP these fragments from the poem 'Cathedral Builders':

Cathedral Builders
They climbed on ladders
hoisted rock into heaven
defied gravity
took up God's house to meet him

And came down to their suppers
lay with their smelly wives
Quarrelled and cuffed the children
Spat, sang, were happy or unhappy.

And every day took to the ladders again
grew greyer, shakier, became less inclined
to (1) . . .

Saw naves sprout arches
Cursed the (2) . . . for their luck
Somehow escaped (3) . . ., got rheumatism,
Decided it was time to give it up,

To leave the spire to others; stood in the crowd
at the consecration,
Envied the fat (4) . . . his warm boots,
Cocked up a squint eye and said (5) . . . .

Tell the students that this is part of a poem about the lives of the old
cathedral builders. Before going on, explain or translate any words
or expressions which might give difficulty, for example: *hoisted,
cuffed, saw naves sprout arches, spire, consecration, cocked up a squint
eye.*

6 Allow time for questions and discussion. Then ask the class to
suggest what was said in the five blank spaces. If you wish, ask the
questions in this way:

– *What did the builders become less inclined to do?*
– *Who did they 'curse for their luck'? Why were they lucky?*
– *What did the builders 'escape'? Was it something worse than
rheumatism?*
– *At the consecration, who did the builders 'envy'?*
– *Why is he wearing 'warm boots'?*
– *When the builders look up at the work they have done (the cathedral
they have built) what do they say?*

7 Listen to the students' suggestions, then give them a copy of the
full text and, if possible, play a recording of the poem.

NOTES

1 If you feel that the poem is too difficult, you could use the prose
text from William Golding: *The Spire*. One of the reasons for
offering a shortened version of the poem (in *In class*, step 5) is that
the main body of the text can easily be understood without much
explanation. The purpose of the shortened text is to stimulate
discussion. The complete text should be easier to understand after
this discussion.

2 In what order should the material be presented? Although it
would seem natural to present the literary text first, and use it as a
basis for developing the discussion topic, this does not always prove
to be the best approach, for two reasons:

a. Students tend to be influenced by the model. If they read the
literary text first, it shapes their thoughts and also constricts their

thinking. Whereas if they first range freely over the topic, they become more receptive to what is said in the text.

b. Students take more interest in a work if they have already contributed something of their own. Much language work is restricted to asking students to comment on texts. But their comment will be much sharper if they have already formulated their own thoughts.

3 *Expanding the topic.* Any discussion topic will naturally stir up thoughts on related themes. For instance, the passages on cathedral builders may lead to discussion of architecture, conservation, home interiors, town planning, traffic regulation, and other related topics. Or, following a different line of thought, to difficult, tiring, or dangerous types of work. You may find that texts with which the students are already familiar (for example 'Night-Shift Workers' in activity 1.5 *Split poem* could be used to stimulate further discussion.

4 Many useful ideas which could be adapted to include literary texts are to be found in Fried-Booth: *Project Work*, in this series.

The long climb back to glory

A line by the 19th century Jesuit poet Gerard Manley Hopkins says, 'There lives the dearest freshness deep down things.' The masons who crafted the medieval cathedrals of Europe knew that first; and their gift was not only to pluck that quality out of the deepest recesses of human insight but to make it visible in the sky and in the air.

In the town which their bishop christened New Sarum, the master masons went further in the purpose—and hazarded more—than almost anyone except the architects of the Pyramids. On foundations four feet deep, a foot above the water table, they built a spire 404 feet high, the tallest in Britain and the second tallest in Europe.

The incredible stone spaceship they left in a Wiltshire water meadow, its spire and pinnacles poised through 650 years for take-off into Deep Heaven, has been an inspiration and friend of every generation since. The funeral procession of its 13th century founder-bishop, Richard Poore, is commemorated in the nave by an effigy worn smooth by human touch. Not long ago WPC Yvonne Fletcher's parents passed it as they followed their girl's funeral procession down the 448-foot stretch of the nave and choir. Salisbury Cathedral projects the first and last concerns of human beings on an epic but identifiable scale.

The chain of testimony to this is unbroken from Sir Christopher Wren, architect of St Paul's, through Constable's painting to the novelist William Golding who wrote 'Fifteen miles away, you can feel the cathedral begin to pull.'

No generation before ours has had reason to expect that anything except the last trump could remove it. What our generation has to face is the forecast that—unless we change our way of life—Salisbury and many other churches, great and small, will be mouldering, defaced and unrecognisable within the lifetimes of our children or grandchildren.

Twelve years ago, a blink of an eyelid in its lifespan, the 'family' of 800 staff and volunteers which clusters round it and cares for it began to realise that their dear friend was almost terminally ill. For some time the faces of the famous 90 statues of saints on the west front had looked as if they were being 'torn by some agent of evil', as the clerk of works Roy Spring puts it. But the statues are, ultimately, decoration. The worst discovery was that the same enemy agent is attacking three sets of stone decorative bands on the outside of the spire. They help hold up the 4,800-ton combined weight of spire and tower.

These bands have been melted in parts from their original eight inch thickness to two inches. Like the faces of the statues, they look as if someone had hurled vitriol at them; and that is what's happening. The modern industrial world has been throwing diluted sulphuric acid—in the form of acid rain—on top of the effects of frost, wind and the other traditional corroders of stonework. Frost is slow, and this artefact can stare down hurricanes. But, thanks to acid rain, the rate of decay has doubled in speed during Roy Spring's 20 years in his job. 'The statues are now just a mass of decayed stone,' he says. The spire would have fallen in an estimated 20 years.

Thirty-five full-time masons have already begun a ten-year task. Even with £75,000 laser machines which cut stone 12 times as fast as a saw, they will still take over a quarter as long to restore mutilated parts of the cathedral as their medieval predecessors did to build it.

This is what the world knows: a cheering picture of devotion and endeavour. What this picture omits is that the acid rain blitz will continue between now and 1992 and thereafter. We shall have to wait till 1991 for the report of a national monitoring by the Building Research Establishment on the impact of acid rain on ancient fabric. Meanwhile York Minster and Lincoln Cathedral are among the great British churches bothered about it. Further afield Cologne Cathedral is being ravaged.

But for Salisbury the background picture is the starkest yet described in Britain. Roy Spring says: 'The decay is accelerating so rapidly that some of the statues added by the Victorians are now in as bad a state as the medieval ones.

'I have repair work mapped out which will take us 30 years to complete. At the end of that 30 years, the acceleration of decay elsewhere is going to be so great that we will have to start all over again on the parts we are restoring now. If we don't do something about acid rain—if the whole of our species doesn't do something about it—not only will we not have any cathedrals left, we won't have a habitable planet.'

It was Roy Spring who first discovered and photographed the damage. In his scholarly but gently deceptive monograph 'Up the Spire' (Cathedral bookshop, 50p), he says, 'The climb to the capstone is one of interest.' Prince Charles among others, has had cause to wince at the understatement. What Mr Spring is talking about is—first—360 steps up to the tower, some of the way with no handrail to break a fall. You pass graffiti commemorating a mason who fell in the 16th century. Then you do about 150 steps up a series of 10 ladders inside the narrowing spire, with no safety net. These end at a storm door. Reaching through it, you manoeuvre round the outside of the spire as it vibrates in the wind and get hold of iron rungs put in by medieval masons. You climb up these the last 40 feet to the capstone and cross.

But how did they come to build so well—compared with us? In a sense, a cathedral builder's 'kit' was available in the year 1220, just as a kit is plainly behind much of the modern housing at Milton Keynes or the unspeakably pseudo-grandiose offices which are now obliterating that old Victorian cathedral of steam, Liverpool Street Station, and are shortly due to obliterate the back of Kings Cross. The medieval kit was shared between master-masons and ordinary masons moving throughout Europe during the centuries when the possibilities of the Moorish arch were being explored with infinite local variations in a burst of building.

Roy Spring thinks of these men, who knew what could and couldn't be done with local stone at heights, as Fred and Charlie. 'I have a phobia about architects who stand back and say "I built this",' he says, 'They didn't. They drew the pictures.'

(*The Guardian*)

SAMPLE TEXT B

Cathedral Builders

They climbed on sketchy ladders towards God,
With winch and pulley hoisted hewn rock into heaven,
Inhabited sky with hammers, defied gravity,
Deified stone, took up God's house to meet Him.

And came down to their suppers and small beer;
Every night slept, lay with their smelly wives,
Quarrelled and cuffed the children, lied,
Spat, sang, were happy or unhappy.

And every day took to the ladders again;
Impeded the rights of way of another summer's
Swallows, grew greyer, shakier, became less inclined
To fix a neighbour's roof of a fine evening.

Saw naves sprout arches, clerestories soar,
Cursed the loud fancy glaziers for their luck,
Somehow escaped the plague, got rheumatism,
Decided it was time to give it up.

To leave the spire to others; stood in the crowd
Well back from the vestments at the consecration,
Envied the fat bishop his warm boots,
Cocked up a squint eye and said, 'I bloody did that'.

(John Ormond: 'Cathedral Builders')

SAMPLE TEXT C

When he woke at dawn next morning, he could hear the rain, and he remembered what the master builder had said. So he prayed among other things for fine weather. But the rain came for three days, with only a half day to follow it of low cloud and soaked air; so that housewives hung what linen there was to wash before smouldering fires that dirtied more linen than they dried; and then there was wind and rain for a week. When he came out of his deanery, cloaked for the hurried passage to the cathedral, he would see the clouds at roof level so that even the battlements of the roof were blurred by them. As for the whole building itself, the bible in stone, it was slimy with water streaming down over moss and lichen and flaking stones. When the rain drizzled, then time was a drizzle, slow and to be endured.

At the crossways of the cathedral there was no more digging. One day, Jocelin stood by the master builder, watched him lower a candle on a string, and saw how water shone at the bottom of the pit. Also, he smelt the pit, and recoiled from it. But the master builder took no account of smells. He stayed where he was, staring gloomily down at the candle. Jocelin became anxious and urgent. He hung by Roger Mason's shoulder.

'What will you do now, my son?'

Roger Mason grunted.

'There's plenty to do.'

He eased himself carefully into the bottom of a corkscrew stair and climbed out of sight; and later, Jocelin heard him moving carefully, a hundred and twenty feet up, by the vaulting.

During this time, the master builder and some of his army worked in the roof over the crossways. They broke up the vaulting so that now if there was any light at all in the crossways and you looked up, you could see rafters. While some men worked there, disappearing into the corkscrew stairs that riddled the walls of the building, to appear later flysize in the triforium, others built scaffolding round the south-east pillar of the crossways. They set ladders from level to level, a spidery construction so that when it was finished the pillar looked like a firtree with the branches cut back. This new work was not without advantage to the services, for the builders could not be heard so easily in the roof. There was little more interruption to the stinking peace of the nave than the occasional blow of a maul at roofheight. Presently ropes began to hang down from the broken vault over the crossways, and stayed there, swinging, as if the building sweating now with damp inside as well as out, had begun to grow some sort of gigantic moss. The ropes were waiting for the beams that would be inched through the gap in the north wall; but they looked like moss and went with the smell. In this dark and wet, it took even Jocelin all his will, to remember that something important was being done; and when a workman fell through the hole above the crossways, and left a scream scored all the way down the air which was so thick it seemed to keep the scream as something mercilessly engraved there, he did not wonder that no miracle interposed between the body and the logical slab of stone that received it.

(William Golding: *The Spire*)

SAMPLE TEXT D

Brickmaking, building and stoneworking

I shall also describe to you the bricklayer . . .When he must be outside in the wind, he lays bricks without a garment. His belt is a cord for his back, a string for his buttocks. His strength has vanished through fatigue and stiffness . . . [and] he eats bread with his fingers, although he washes himself but once a day.

Labourers in the building trades are pictured in the tomb of Rekhmirē. The task of laying bricks is here given to Nubian captives, an interesting parallel to the fate of the Children of Israel in the Bible (*Exodus* 1:13–14). On the left, a man is seen filling jars with water while, further right, others are hoeing the ground and filling baskets with earth. After mixing these two substances with straw to bind the mass, the mud is poured into wooden moulds and left in the sun to dry. Then, as now, most of the bricks were not fired, but were transported to the work-site as soon as the surface hardened, either in quantity with the aid of a yoke or a few at a time. Domestic architecture depended mainly on unfired bricks for the shell of a building, but any large construction would be made of stone, and its interior filled with earth as successive courses were added, or with a series of mudbrick ramps giving access. What appears to be a stone building partly obscured by such a ramp is seen on the extreme right in the tomb of Rekhmirē. Another good example is still preserved at Karnak, against the east face of the south wing of the first pylon, found here because the building remained unfinished in antiquity.

Building in stone is also illustrated in the tomb of Rekhmirē, in the two registers below the brickmaking scenes. Ships laden with stone are first seen on the bottom, arriving from the quarries. Masons are next seen chipping at the blocks or stretching cords across their surfaces to see whether they are truly smooth. Above, gangs of men are seen hauling huge blocks of granite with the aid of ropes and levers, while at the right sculptors shape the hard stone into statues. Since at this time the Egyptians still had only soft metals – copper and bronze – at their disposal, the required shaping of the stone was done with dolerite balls which were also used to literally pound the granite loose from the bed of the quarry: a good example of their patience is the unfinished obelisk in the granite quarries on the east bank at Aswan. Transport of granite columns, pictured on a block from the causeway to the pyramid of King Unis at Saqqara, fades into insignificance before the conveyance of Queen Hatshepsut's great obelisks down to Thebes: the monuments are settled on the decks of two enormous barges, with groups of tugboats to guide these monsters downstream, and the profusion of masts and cables vividly evokes what must have been an astounding technological spectacle in its day.

In addition to statuary, the Egyptians excelled from earliest times in making finely crafted stone vessels. Examples of their art fill the world's museums and the perfection they achieved is all the more amazing in that the only drill available was a cumbersome instrument: consisting of a forked shaft made of hard stone, it was turned by crank attached to its upper end, with stones lashed to the handle to provide greater stability. Even so, great strength and stamina must have been required of the operator. This process, as well as polishing vases with a stone scraper, is pictured in many tombs, both of Old and New Kingdom date.

(*The Penguin Guide to Ancient Egypt*)

SAMPLE TEXT E

My Busconductor

My busconductor tells me
he only has one kidney
and that may soon go on strike
through overwork.
Each busticket
takes on now a different shape
and texture.
He holds a ninepenny single
as if it were a rose
and puts the shilling in his bag
as a child into a gasmeter.
His thin lips
have no quips
for fat factorygirls
and he ignores
the drunk who snores
and the oldman who talks to himself
and gets off at the wrong stop.
He goes gently to the bedroom
of the bus
to collect
and watch familiar shops and pubs passby
(perhaps for the last time?)
The sameold streets look different now
more distinct
as through new glasses.
And the sky
was it ever so blue?

And all the time
deepdown in the deserted busshelter of his mind
he thinks about his journey nearly done.
One day he'll clock on and never clock off
or clock off and never clock on.

(Roger McGough: 'My Busconductor')

3.5 Discussion topics 2: observation

LEVEL

Lower intermediate

TIME

20 – 30 minutes

PREPARATION

1 For this activity, you will need descriptive material, particularly
passages which evoke a strong sense of place. These may be
descriptions of cities, streets, landscapes, interiors, and so on.
Such descriptions can easily be found in novels and short stories.

Other useful sources are diaries, autobiographies, letters, and travel books.

2 Select one or two short passages which you feel would stimulate the students to think further about their own powers of observation. Two examples are given in the sample texts. The approach described below relates directly to the extract from Isherwood: *A Berlin Diary* (sample text A).

3 Make enough copies of the text you have chosen for one third of the class.

IN CLASS

1 Write up on the board the words *From my window*. Ask the students, working individually, to note down what they can see from their own window, or what can be seen from any window in their home.

After five minutes, ask them to form groups of three and to exchange observations. Remind them that in addition to the things they see they could also mention the people who regularly pass by or who stand around in the street.

2 Read aloud or play a recording of the passage from *A Berlin Diary*. After the reading give each group a copy of the text.

3 Draw the students' attention to these words in the text:
I am a camera with its shutter open, quite passive, recording, not thinking. Recording the man shaving at the window opposite and the woman in the kimono washing her hair. Some day all this will have to be developed, carefully printed, fixed.

4 Ask the students, in their groups of three, to imagine that they are 'a camera with its shutter open' in their own town, and that they are going to take photographs of their town in order to remember it as it is.

Each group should draw up a list of at least five 'shots' (photographs) they would like to take. Ask the students to consider the following points in deciding on their shots:
– *What is the focal point of the picture? What detail(s) would the eye be drawn to? What would there be in the background?*
– *At what time of day would you take the picture?*
– *Would there be any people or animals in the picture?*
– *What would be your reason for taking the picture?*
– *Does the scene have any personal associations?*

5 Allow at least ten minutes for discussion of the shots. Then ask each group to exchange ideas with another.

6 *Round-up discussion.* Did any groups choose the same or similar shots? Which suggestions were the most striking or unusual? Which would be the most difficult to take?

NOTES

1 Descriptive passages in literature often wash over us without leaving any clear impression. This may be because in a foreign language we do not understand the words (words like 'dirty plaster frontages embossed with scroll-work'), or because the scene

described is too remote from our own experience, or because we cannot see in our minds what the writer sees. For reasons such as these, students often find descriptive passages difficult to work with.

This is why we have placed the main emphasis in this activity on the students' own powers of observation. They will certainly be able to talk about what they themselves see every day. And to do this, they do not need to use 'literary language'. Sample text A is not intended to be studied for its use of language, but rather for the suggestive power of the central thought 'I am a camera'.

2 In *In class*, steps 4 and 5, the students should be encouraged to use language as precisely as possible. In describing their shots, they will, for instance, need to make frequent use of prepositions (*at, next to, beneath, under, beside*). If you wish, write up on the board a check-list of prepositions and adverbs they may need. You might also remind them that in the discussion it would be natural to use the conditional form: 'Our first picture *would show* the greengrocer pulling down his shutters in the evening. . .'

Note also that, although the students do not have to refer back to the literary text, they may like to borrow ideas from it, for instance: '. . . soon the whistling will begin. Young men are calling their girls.'

SAMPLE TEXT A   (The author is reflecting on life as it goes on beyond his own window.)

From my window, the deep solemn massive street. Cellar-shops where the lamps burn all day, under the shadow of top-heavy balconied façades, dirty plaster frontages embossed with scroll-work and heraldic devices. The whole district is like this: street leading into street of houses like shabby monumental safes crammed with the tarnished valuables and second-hand furniture of a bankrupt middle class.

I am a camera with its shutter open, quite passive, recording, not thinking. Recording the man shaving at the window opposite and the woman in the kimono washing her hair. Some day, all this will have to be developed, carefully printed, fixed.

At eight o'clock in the evening the house-doors will be locked. The children are having supper. The shops are shut. The electric sign is switched on over the night-bell of the little hotel on the corner, where you can hire a room by the hour. And soon the whistling will begin. Young men are calling their girls. Standing down there in the cold, they whistle up at the lighted windows of warm rooms where the beds are already turned down for the night. They want to be let in. Their signals echo down the deep hollow street, lascivious and private and sad. Because of the whistling, I do not care to stay here in the evenings. It reminds me that I am in a foreign city, alone, far from home. Sometimes I determine not to listen to it, pick up a book, try to read. But soon a call is sure to sound, so piercing, so insistent, so despairingly human, that at last

I have to get up and peep through the slats of the venetian blind to make quite sure that it is not – as I know very well it could not possibly be – for me.

(Christopher Isherwood: *A Berlin Diary*)

SAMPLE TEXT B

(The author is observing school children from the window of his flat, which overlooks the school.)

I used to watch the school across the road; the kids coming and going in the morning and afternoon and streaming into the playground at breaks. It was getting near the time they broke up for the summer; then the school would close for good and the demolition men would move in. Through one of the tall windows, opposite but a little below our room, I could see the teacher standing before the blackboard, but because of the level of the window I couldn't see his seated class. It looked as if he was speaking and gesticulating to no one. I watched him struggling to communicate with his invisible audience, waving his arms and raising his voice, and I felt sorry for him.

In the third week of July the school closed and the din from the playground ceased. Almost immediately several council vans turned up and took away the interior furnishings. Some of the equipment in the kitchen was dismantled and some old fold-up desks were stacked in the playgound. Then the vans drove away, leaving the school like a forlorn fort amidst the besieging demolition sites. I asked myself if the kids who had gone to the school cared that it was going to be flattened. I saw some of them sometimes, playing games over the demolition sites, rooting about amongst the rubbish heaps, setting fire to things and being chased off by the site workers.

Then one day, only about a fortnight after the school closed, there were two boys in the school playground. They were walking around, looking at the heap of desks and peering through the wired ground-floor windows. I was puzzled as to how they'd got there. Then I saw the head of a third boy – and a fourth – appear over the playground wall in the far left corner where it joined the school building. There seemed to be a loose section of the wire netting above the wall, which could be lifted back and squeezed under, and although the wall was a good ten feet, the pile of desks in the corner made it possible, even for a boy of eleven or so, to lower himself down. In a short while there were five boys in the playground, mooching about in grubby jeans and tee-shirts.

Their first impulse was to ransack everything. I watched them try to force their way into the school building through the big door from the playground. When this failed, they picked up some old lengths of piping left by the council workers and, poking them through the metal grilles over the windows, began smashing the panes. They used the same bits of piping to hack up lumps of asphalt from the playground, which they hurled at the upper windows. The noise they made was lost in the general noise of demolition. One of them climbed up onto the roof of one of the two small lavatory buildings abutting the school wall, and with the aid of a drain pipe, tried to reach the first floor windows – but climbed down when he realised he would be visible from street level. Then they started to dismantle the lavatories themselves – crude little temporary buildings made from flimsy prefabricated materials, with corrugated asbestos roofs.

I wondered whether these were the same kids who broke into the tenement and set fire to the litter on the stairs. They came the next day, and the day after that, and the next day again. It seemed odd that they should return at all to the school – like released prisoners going voluntarily back to prison.

(Graham Swift: *Learning to Swim*)

3.6 Discussion topics 3: memories

LEVEL	**All levels**
TIME	**45 – 60 minutes**

PREPARATION

1 For this activity, you will need a selection of four to six texts relating to childhood memories and experiences. In making your selection, look out in particular for passages which touch on themes and aspects of life which are part of the common experience of children everywhere, and with which your own students could readily identify, for instance, evocations of childhood dreams and fears, descriptions of home, family, friends and neighbours, memories of games, parties, formal occasions, or festivals.

Suitable texts are not hard to find. Novels and short stories abound in childhood recollections. So, too, do the autobiographies of writers such as Graham Greene, John Osborne, and V. S. Pritchett.

2 Make enough copies of the texts you have chosen so that each group of four students has a set of two texts.

3 Ask the students to bring to class any objects or pictures associated with their childhood (an old toy or doll, a faded photograph, a favourite book).

IN CLASS

1 *Warm-up discussion.* Ask the students to form groups of four, and to show each other the objects they have brought to class. In turn, they describe any memories associated with these objects.

2 The students remain in their groups of four. On the board or OHP, display a number of stimulus questions, such as the following:

When you were young:

– *What food did you most like/hate?*
– *Was there a particular time of day you liked best/least?*
– *What smells did you associate with home?*
– *Who, or what, were you most frightened of?*
– *Did you have a favourite hiding-place?*

– *What kind of games did you play, or invent?*
– *Were there any words (in your own language) that you did not understand, or could not pronounce properly?*
– *What special occasions (birthdays, festivals, visits to relatives, going to church/mosque/temple) did you enjoy or dislike?*
– *Did you have any pet animals?*
– *What clothes did you most/least like to wear?*
– *Which person in your family or neighbourhood could you talk to most freely?*
– *What task, at home or at school, did you find most difficult to do?*
– *Were you ever punished? What for?*
– *What did you like most/least about the family routine (meal-times, bed-time, washing-up)*
– *What did you want to be when you 'grew up'?*

3 In their groups, the students discuss their responses to the stimulus questions.

4 Give each group any two of the texts you have chosen (or of those given under sample texts). Ask the students to read through the passages quickly and to note down any remarks, comments, or descriptions that remind them of comments they made in their earlier discussion. They should also pick out any details in the passages which remind them of things they had forgotten to mention.

(Optional) Each group exchanges texts with a group which was working on different passages. Again, they discuss how the passages relate to their own experiences.

5 *Listening*. To round off the session, read out or play a recording of the extract from Dickens: *Great Expectations*. This type of listening activity need not be followed by discussion unless you particularly want to explore the text.

NOTES

1 In this activity everyone is equal. We all have childhood memories, and only we know what those memories are. The students, then, can speak without any fear of 'being wrong'. They can also choose what they would like to mention, and what they would prefer to hold back. Starting discussion, therefore, should not be a problem. What may be a problem, however, is controlling the language of discussion. Since the students will be talking about their own past experiences, they will naturally be tempted to use the mother tongue.

One way of encouraging the students to use English rather than the mother tongue in their discussion is to ask each group to note down (in English) some of their responses to the stimulus questions. Then, extend *In class*, step 3 by asking each group to read out to the class a selection of their responses.

2 The texts which you distribute (*In class*, step 4) will also help to establish the language of discussion as English, because the students will be relating certain lines and expressions back to their earlier discussion.

These texts are not intended to be closely studied. Their function is to stimulate further thought and talk. The main focus remains the discussion of childhood memories, in which the texts serve as an outside point of reference.

3 *Listening.* There is a time when students need to be able to relax and enjoy literature without being required to comment on it. After such a long oral activity, the students may welcome the chance to just sit back and listen. (See also 4.6 – 4.9 *Listening.*)

4 Further ideas on the association of childhood memories and literature are to be found in Hedge: *Writing,* in this series.

SAMPLE TEXT A

My father was a very clean man, who never took less than two baths a day. One day I came home from school and found him wearing a white towelling dressing-gown and sitting on the closed lavatory seat in the bathroom. My mother was squeezing out his toothpaste. She found his hand and put the toothbrush into it. Then she guided his hand towards his mouth. That was the first time I saw that he was totally blind.

Eyesight was a problem for both of us. Up to the age of five I enjoyed the privileges of myopia, seeing the world in a glorious haze like an Impressionist painting. My contemporaries appeared blurred and attractive, grown-ups loomed in vague magnificence. I went daily to school and kept my eyes politely on the blackboard where I could see only chalky confusion. After a year of this my mother noticed that my education was at a standstill and sent me to the oculist: the world sprang at me in hideous reality, full of people with open pores, blackheads and impetigo. A deep-focus moustache appeared on an art mistress whom I had considered beautiful. Flinching from this unusual clarity I went to school and sat in my usual place at the morning assembly, unrecognizable in a nose-pinching pair of wire-framed specs. The headmaster, whose awareness of his pupils was always somewhat vague, thought that this bespectacled intruder was a new boy. As I was too shy to disillusion him, I was put back in the bottom class to restart my unpromising academic career. I suppose I had become a new person, one who looked on life and actually saw it; but when faced with anything I am really reluctant to see, a pornographic film in the course of business, or an animal killed and plastered across the road, I still have the defence of taking off my glasses and returning the world to the safe blur of childhood.

In the years before I could see clearly my father was not yet blind.

(John Mortimer: *Clinging to the Wreckage*)

SAMPLE TEXT B

I was thrown into the society of young people. My cousins were none of them, I believe, any longer children, but they were youths and maidens busily engaged in various personal interests, all collected in a hive of wholesome family energy. Everybody was very kind to me, and I sank back, after the strain of so many months, into mere childhood again. This long visit to my cousins at Clifton must have been very delightful: I am dimly aware that it was; yet I remember but few of incidents. My memory, so clear and vivid about earlier solitary times, now in all this society becomes blurred and vague.

The life of a child is so brief, its impressions are so illusory and fugitive, that it is as difficult to record its history as it would be to design a morning cloud sailing before the wind. It is short, as we count shortness in after years, when the drag of lead pulls down to earth the foot that used to flutter with a winged impetuosity. But in memory, my childhood was long, long with interminable hours, hours with the pale cheek pressed against the window-pane, hours of mechanical and repeated lonely 'games', which had lost their savour, and were kept going by sheer inertness. Not unhappy, not fretful, but long, – long, long. It seems to me, as I look back to the life in the motherless Islington house, as I resumed it in that slow eighth year of my life, that time had ceased to move. There was a whole age between one tick of the eight-day clock in the hall, and the next tick. When the milkman went his rounds in our grey street, it seemed as though he would never disappear again. There was no past and no future for me, and the present felt as though it were sealed up in a Leyden jar. Even my dreams were interminable, and hung stationary from the nightly sky.

(Edmund Gosse: *Father and Son*)

SAMPLE TEXT C

We had oil lamps and a shallow tin bath, which was filled with water from the well. Going to the loo meant an icy journey to the end of the garden and sitting on a bench carved by Mr Mullard. Almost before you were finished he would be behind the shed with a spade, ready to dig and spread among his vegetables.

Apart from the Mullards my great friend was Iris Jones, the gardener's daughter from the cottage along the common. She was exactly my age and we would meet very early in the mornings, and I would steal necklaces for her from Woolworth's. All one summer we made houses on the common, enjoying the sharp, musky smell of the bracken, furnishing our homes with chipped Coronation mugs and bottomless, rusty saucepans which we found in the local tip.

. . . I had a recurring dream which was that at the age of nine I should be taken out and hanged. In my dream I protested to my father at this gloomy destiny, but he seemed not to hear. When I spoke to my mother she gave me her usual large-eyed, reasonable smile and told me that it was something that happened to all small boys and it was really nothing to worry about. I now feel sure that what I was looking forward to as the morning of my execution was my being sent away to school.

(John Mortimer: *Clinging to the Wreckage*)

SAMPLE TEXT D   Following the long-established example of my father's parents, we even had prayers before breakfast, during which performance everybody – from my mother, who perturbedly watched the boiling coffee-machine on the table, to the maids who shuffled uneasily in their chairs while the postman banged at the front door and the milkman thundered at the back – presented an aspect of inattentive agitation. The ceremony frequently ended in a tempestuous explosion on the part of my father, since Edward was almost always late, and could never say the Lord's Prayer as rapidly as the others.

(Vera Brittain: *Testament of Youth*)

LISTENING TEXT   Though she called me 'boy' so often, and with a carelessness that was far from complimentary, she was of about my own age. She seemed much older than I, of course, being a girl, and beautiful and self-possessed; and she was as scornful of me as if she had been one-and-twenty, and a queen.

We went into the house by a side door – the great front entrance had two chains across it outside – and the first thing I noticed was, that the passages were all dark, and that she had left a candle burning there. She took it up, and we went through more passages and up a staircase, and still it was all dark, and only the candle lighted us.

At last we came to the door of a room, and she said, 'Go in.'

I answered, more in shyness than politeness, 'After you, miss.'

To this, she returned: 'Don't be ridiculous, boy; I am not going in.' And scornfully walked away, and – what was worse – took the candle with her.

This was very uncomfortable, and I was half afraid. However, the only thing to be done being to knock at the door, I knocked, and was told from within to enter. I entered, therefore, and found myself in a pretty large room, well lighted with wax candles. No glimpse of daylight was to be seen in it. It was a dressing-room, as I supposed from the furniture, though much of it was of forms and uses then quite unknown to me. But prominent in it was a draped table with a gilded looking-glass, and that I made out at first sight to be a fine lady's dressing-table.

Whether I should have made out this object so soon, if there had been no fine lady sitting at it, I cannot say. In an arm-chair, with an elbow resting on the table and her head leaning on that hand, sat the strangest lady I have ever seen, or shall ever see.

She was dressed in rich materials – satins, and lace, and silks – all of white. Her shoes were white. And she had a long white veil dependent from her hair, and she had bridal flowers in her hair, but her hair was white. Some bright jewels sparkled on her neck and on her hands, and some other jewels lay sparkling on the table. Dresses, less splendid than the dress she wore, and half-packed trunks, were scattered about. She had not quite finished dressing, for she had but one shoe on – the other was on the table near her hand – her veil was but half arranged, her watch and chain were not put on, and some lace for her bosom lay with those trinkets, and with her handkerchief, and gloves, and some flowers, and a prayerbook, all confusedly heaped about the looking-glass.

It was not in the first few moments that I saw all these things, though I saw more of them in the first moments than might be supposed. But, I saw that everything within my view which ought to be white, had been white long ago, and had lost its lustre, and was faded and yellow. I saw that the bride within the bridal dress had withered like the dress, and like the flowers, and had no brightness left but the brightness of her sunken eyes. I saw that the dress had been put upon the rounded figure of a young woman, and that the figure upon which it now hung loose, had shrunk to skin and bone. Once, I had been taken to see some ghastly waxwork at the Fair, representing I know not what impossible personage lying in state. Once, I had been taken to one of our old marsh churches to see a skeleton in the ashes of a rich dress, that had been dug out of a vault under the church pavement. Now, waxwork and skeleton seemed to have dark eyes that moved and looked at me. I should have cried out, if I could.

'Who is it?' said the lady at the table.

'Pip, ma'am.'

'Pip?'

'Mr Pumblechook's boy, ma'am. Come – to play.'

'Come nearer; let me look at you. Come close.'

It was when I stood before her, avoiding her eyes, that I took note of the surrounding objects in detail, and saw that her watch had stopped at twenty minutes to nine, and that a clock in the room had stopped at twenty minutes to nine.

'Look at me,' said Miss Havisham. 'You are not afraid of a woman who has never seen the sun since you were born?'

I regret to state that I was not afraid of telling the enormous lie comprehended in the answer 'No.'

'Do you know what I touch here?' she said, laying her hands, one upon the other, on her left side.

'Yes, ma'am.' (It made me think of the young man.)

'What do I touch?'

'Your heart.'

'Broken!'

She uttered the word with an eager look, and with strong emphasis, and with a weird smile that had a kind of boast in it. Afterwards, she kept her hands there for a little while, and slowly took them away as if they were heavy.

'I am tired,' said Miss Havisham. 'I want diversion, and I have done with men and women. Play.'

I think it will be conceded by my most disputatious reader, that she could hardly have directed an unfortunate boy to do anything in the wide world more difficult to be done under the circumstances.

'I sometimes have sick fancies,' she went on, 'and I have a sick fancy that I want to see some play. There, there!' with an impatient movement of the fingers of her right hand; 'play, play, play!'

For a moment, with the fear of my sister's working me before my eyes, I had a desperate idea of starting round the room in the assumed character of Mr Pumblechook's chaise-cart. But, I felt myself so unequal to the performance that I gave it up, and stood looking at Miss Havisham in what I suppose she took for a dogged manner, inasmuch as she said, when we had taken a good look at each other:

'Are you sullen and obstinate?'

'No, ma'am, I am very sorry for you, and very sorry I can't play just now. If you complain of me I shall get into trouble with my sister, so I would do it if I could; but it's so new here, and so strange, and so fine – and melancholy –' I stopped, fearing I might say too much, or had already said it, and we took another look at each other.

Before she spoke again, she turned her eyes from me, and looked at the dress she wore, and at the dressing-table, and finally at herself in the looking-glass.

'So new to him,' she muttered, 'so old to me; so strange to him, so familiar to me; so melancholy to both of us! Call Estella.'

As she was still looking at the reflection of herself, I thought she was still talking to herself, and kept quiet.

'Call Estella,' she repeated, flashing a look at me. 'You can do that. Call Estella. At the door.'

To stand in the dark in a mysterious passage of an unknown house, bawling Estella to a scornful young lady neither visible nor responsive, and feeling it a dreadful liberty so to roar out her name, was almost as bad as playing to order. But, she answered at last, and her light came along the dark passage like a star.

Miss Havisham beckoned her to come close, and took up a jewel from the table, and tried its effect upon her fair young bosom and against her pretty brown hair. 'Your own, one day, my dear, and you will use it well. Let me see you play cards with this boy.'

'With this boy! Why, he is a common labouring-boy!'

I thought I overheard Miss Havisham answer – only it seemed so unlikely – 'Well? You can break his heart.'

'What do you play, boy?' asked Estella of myself, with the greatest disdain.

'Nothing but beggar my neighbour, miss.'

'Beggar him,' said Miss Havisham to Estella. So we sat down to cards.

It was then I began to understand that everything in the room had stopped, like the watch and the clock, a long time ago. I noticed that Miss Havisham put down the jewel exactly on the spot from which she had taken it up. As Estella dealt the cards, I glanced at the dressing-table again, and saw that the shoe upon it, once white, now yellow, had never been worn. I glanced down at the foot from which the shoe was absent, and saw that the silk stocking, once white, now yellow, had been trodden ragged. Without this arrest of everything, this standing still of all the pale decayed objects, not even the withered bridal dress on the collapsed form could have looked like grave-clothes, or the long veil so like a shroud.

So she sat, corpse-like, as we played at cards; the frillings and trimmings on her bridal dress, looking like earthy paper. I knew nothing then, of the discoveries that are occasionally made of bodies buried in ancient times, which fall to powder in the moment of being distinctly seen; but, I have often thought since, that she must have looked as if the admission of the natural light of day would have struck her to dust.

'He calls the knaves, Jacks, this boy!' said Estella with disdain, before our first game was out. 'And what coarse hands he has! And what thick boots!'

I had never thought of being ashamed of my hands before; but I began to consider them a very indifferent pair. Her contempt for me was so strong, and it became infectious, and I caught it.

She won the game, and I dealt. I misdealt, as was only natural, when I knew she was lying in wait for me to do wrong; and she denounced me for a stupid, clumsy labouring-boy.

'You say nothing of her,' remarked Miss Havisham to me, as she looked on. 'She says many hard things of you, but you say nothing of her. What do you think of her?'

'I don't like to say,' I stammered.

'Tell me in my ear,' said Miss Havisham, bending down.

'I think she is very proud,' I replied, in a whisper.

'Anything else?'

'I think she is very pretty.'

'Anything else?'

'I think she is very insulting.' (She was looking at me then with a look of supreme aversion.)

'Anything else?'

'I think I should like to go home.'

'And never see her again, though she is so pretty?'

'I am not sure that I shouldn't like to see her again, but I should like to go home now.'

'You shall go soon,' said Miss Havisham, aloud. 'Play the game out.'

Saving for the one weird smile at first, I should have felt almost sure that Miss Havisham's face could not smile. It had dropped into a watchful and brooding expression – most likely when all the things about her had become transfixed – and it looked as if nothing could ever lift it up again. Her chest had dropped, so that she stooped; and her voice had dropped, so that she spoke low, and with a dead lull upon her; altogether, she had the appearance of having dropped, body and soul, within and without, under the weight of a crushing blow.

I played the game to an end with Estella, and she beggared me. She threw the cards down on the table when she had won them all, as if she despised them for having been won of me.

'When shall I have you here again?' said Miss Havisham. 'Let me think.'

I was beginning to remind her that to-day was Wednesday, when she checked me with her former impatient movement of the fingers of her right hand.

'There, there! I know nothing of days of the week; I know nothing of weeks of the year. Come again after six days. You hear?'

'Yes, ma'am.'

'Estella, take him down. Let him have something to eat, and let him roam and look about him while he eats. Go, Pip.'

(Charles Dickens: *Great Expectations*)

3.7 Discussion topics 4: sound and silence

LEVEL Intermediate to advanced

TIME 30 – 45 minutes

PREPARATION 1 Make a selection of texts which focus strongly on sound: pleasant or irritating sounds, sudden noises, silences which are soothing or disturbing.

2 Prepare enough copies for one third of the class.

IN CLASS 1 *Warm-up discussion.* Ask the students to form groups of three. Write up on the board two column headings:

Irritating sounds Pleasant sounds.

Under each of these headings, the students then note their suggestions. For instance:

Irritating sounds:
- *the thump, thump of heavy rock music from the flat above you at 3a.m.*
- *the sound of somebody nervously clicking a ball-point pen, jangling keys or coins in their pocket, cracking their fingers, sucking their teeth*
- *dogs barking at the full moon, cats calling for their mates in February, parrots or children repeating the same words over and over again*
- *the screech of chalk on the blackboard, the whine of a dentist's drill, the dripping of a tap at night*
- *whispering, giggling, sniggering, wheezing, coughing*
- *cuckoo clocks, alarm clocks, grandfather clocks, chiming door-bells, cracked records, fuzzy telephone lines*
  etc.

Pleasant sounds:
- *the hissing and crackling of a log fire on a winter evening*
- *the patter of raindrops after a long dry spell*
- *the ringing of bells, from a church or temple*
- *cicadas/crickets/frogs on a summer evening*
- *fountains splashing*
- *the swish of skis on firm snow*
- *the phone ringing just when you thought 'he' or 'she' would not call*
- *the sudden 'pop' of a wine cork*
- *the clatter of coins when you win the jackpot on a fruit-machine*
  etc.

2 Each group joins another to compare notes. The students should not just read out their notes to each other. They should also explain why they find particular sounds pleasant or irritating.

3 Ask the students to return to their former groups. Give each group a copy of the extract from the poem 'Silence'. After reading the poem, the students should add ten lines of their own, following

the same basic pattern, beginning each line with the words *There is the silence of*..., or *and*...*of*... (The lines do not need to rhyme or to have poetic rhythm; they are just further thoughts.)

4 (Optional) Ask the students to work in groups of three. Give each group a copy of the extract from D. H. Lawrence: 'The Fox' (see sample texts). Ask them to imagine that they are producing a filmed version of the story for television. The film should follow the text as closely as possible. The task of the groups is to mark all parts of the text which would be reflected in the sound–track of the film.

This means that they should mark all passages where sound would be needed, and all passages where silence would be best. For instance:

Sound: There was a commotion everywhere. The fowls were scuffling and crawking, the ducks were quark-quarking.

Silence: He gathered all his vision into a concentrated spark, and saw the shadow of the fox, the fox creeping on his belly through the gate. There he went, on his belly, like a snake.

5 *Class discussion*. First, ask the students to call out those parts of the text which they think should be reflected on the sound-track. Then, if possible, play a recording of the extract. After listening, discuss any points of difference or disagreement.

NOTES

1 The theme of 'Sound and silence' is just one of many similar themes which can be explored using literature as the basic material for discussion. In addition to the sense of hearing, we could also consider the senses of taste, touch, smell, and sight or vision. These sensory themes have two great advantages:

a. All students can speak about them from personal experience.

b. Suitable supporting texts can easily be found: the senses and sensuality are part of the fabric of literature.

2 As in many other activities, it is important that the students should first discuss the theme before coming to the texts. Otherwise, their thoughts will be too much influenced by what they have read.

The texts themselves can be introduced in many ways other than those suggested in the description of the activity. You could, for instance, focus on vocabulary by presenting the students with short passages containing 'sound' words (*rumble, grate, rasp, thud, shrill, dull, muffled, raucous*). Then ask the students to decide from the context what kind of sound is described. Is it:

– *short/long, continuous/interrupted?*
– *soft/loud, harsh/gentle, weak/strong?*
– *slow/sudden, deep/shrill?*
– *soothing/menacing?*
    etc.

Further ideas can be found in Maley and Duff: *Sounds Intriguing* and *The Inward Ear*.

Silence

I have known the silence of the stars and of the sea,
And the silence of the city when it pauses,
And the silence for which music alone finds the word,
And the silence of the woods before the winds of spring begin,

And the silence of the sick
When their eyes roam about the room . . .

There is the silence of a great hatred,
And the silence of a great love,
And the silence of a deep peace of mind,
And the silence of an embittered friendship . . .

There is the silence of defeat.
There is the silence of those unjustly punished;
And the silence of the dying whose hand
Suddenly grips yours.
There is the silence between father and son,
When the father cannot explain his life,
Even though he be misunderstood for it.

There is the silence that comes between husband and wife.
There is the silence of those who have failed;
And the vast silence that covers
Broken nations and vanquished leaders.

(Edgar Lee Masters: 'Silence')

The Fox

He skirted the fence, peering through the darkness with dilated eyes that seemed to be able to grow black and full of sight in the dark, like a cat's. An owl was slowly and mournfully whooing round a great oak-tree. He stepped stealthily with his gun, listening, listening, watching.

As he stood under the oaks of the wood-edge he heard the dogs from the neighbouring cottage up the hill yelling suddenly and startlingly, and the wakened dogs from the farms around barking answer. And suddenly, it seemed to him England was little and tight, he felt the landscape was constricted even in the dark, and that there were too many dogs in the night, making a noise like a fence of sound, like the network of English hedges netting the view. He felt the fox didn't have a chance. For it must be the fox that had started all this hullabaloo.

Why not watch for him, anyhow! He would, no doubt, be coming sniffing round. The lad walked downhill to where the farmstead with its few pine-trees crouched blackly. In the angle of the long shed, in the black dark, he crouched down. He knew the fox would be coming. It seemed to him it would be the last of the foxes in this loudly barking, thick-voiced England, tight with innumerable little houses.

He sat a long time with his eyes fixed unchanging upon the open gateway, where a little light seemed to fall from the stars or from the horizon, who knows. He was sitting on a log in a dark corner with the gun across his knees. The pine-trees snapped. Once a chicken fell off its perch in the barn with a loud crawk and cackle and commotion that startled him, and he stood up, watching with all his eyes, thinking it might be a rat. But he *felt* it was nothing. So he sat down again with the gun on his knees and his hands tucked in to keep them warm, and his eyes fixed unblinking on the pale reach of the open gateway. He felt he could smell the hot, sickly, rich smell of live chickens on the cold air.

And then – a shadow. A sliding shadow in the gateway. He gathered all his vision into a concentrated spark, and saw the shadow of the fox, the fox creeping on his belly through the gate. There he went, on his belly, like a snake. The boy smiled to himself and brought the gun to his shoulder. He knew quite well what would happen. He knew the fox would go to where the fowl-door was boarded up, and sniff there. He knew he would lie there for a minute, sniffing the fowls within. And then he would start again prowling under the edge of the old barn, waiting to get in.

The fowl-door was at the top of a slight incline. Soft, soft as a shadow the fox slid up this incline, and crouched with his nose to the boards. And at the same moment there was the awful crash of a gun reverberating between the old buildings, as if all the night had gone smash. But the boy watched keenly. He saw even the white belly of the fox as the beast beat his paws in death. So he went forward.

There was a commotion everywhere. The fowls were scuffling and crawking, the ducks were quark-quarking, the pony had stamped wildly to his feet. But the fox was on his side, struggling in his last tremors. The boy bent over him and smelt his foxy smell.

There was a sound of a window opening upstairs, then March's voice calling:

'Who is it?'

'It's me,' said Henry; 'I've shot the fox.'

(D. H. Lawrence: 'The Fox')

3.8 Discussion topics 5: the Underground

LEVEL   Intermediate to advanced

TIME   25 minutes

PREPARATION   1 Select four to six short poems (maximum length fourteen lines) which might be suitable for display in the Underground (*métro*) or some other form of public transport. In sample texts A, at the end of the printed poems you will find an example of a poem which was displayed in the London Underground.

2 Make enough copies for one quarter of the class.

3 Prepare a selection of six to eight advertisements similar to those usually seen in trains and buses.

4 Ask the students to bring to class a copy of a poem they particularly like, either in English or in their own language.

IN CLASS

1 Display the advertisements you have collected (see *Preparation*, step 3) so that all the students can see them. Ask the students to imagine that they are travelling by train or bus, and to pick out the picture or advertisement which would be most likely to capture their attention. Allow only one minute for this.

2 Now, cover or remove the pictures. Ask the students to form groups of four. They should discuss which pictures remain most strongly in their minds, and try to recreate them in words and images in as much detail as possible.

3 Show the pictures again, and allow time for discussion of the missing details.

4 Give each group copies of the poems you have chosen (see *Preparation*, step 1). Ask the students to decide which of the poems they would most like to see displayed in an underground train, or in a bus, why they chose it, and whether they have strong reasons for not choosing the others. Allow time for discussion, then ask the students, as a single group, to indicate their personal preferences.

5 Circulate the poems the students themselves have brought (see *Preparation*, step 4). Ask them to decide which, if any, of the new poems they would like to see displayed.

NOTES

1 This is a flexible activity, in which the literary texts might be introduced at any chosen stage. We have suggested using the poems as a starting point from which the students can work outwards towards discussion of the wider theme. However, it would be equally valid to begin with the discussion (see *Variation*) and then work back towards the poems (see *In class*).

2 Many works of literature contain vivid descriptions of travel by public transport. Suitable passages could be found in Dickens: *The Pickwick Papers*; Guy de Maupassant: *Boule de Suif*; Malcolm Bradbury: *Rates of Exchange*, not to mention the novels of Graham Greene and the travel works of Paul Theroux.

3 See also: 3.1 *Picture stories*, and 3.4–3.5 *Discussion topics*.

SOURCES

Sources of the poems in sample texts A:

1 W. B. Yeats   4 Catherine Woods
2 Alan Jackson   5 Alan Duff
3 D. H. Lawrence   6 Charles Reznikoff

VARIATION   **Extension**

TIME   **60 minutes**

PREPARATION   If you wish to distribute texts, prepare enough copies for one quarter of the class.

IN CLASS   1 The activity can be extended along the lines of 3.4 *Discussion topics 1*. In sample texts B you will find three prose texts which could be used as supplementary material for discussion.

2 For developing the topic, we would suggest the following approach:

WARM-UP   1 *Warm-up discussion*. Write up on the board or OHP the heading:

Travelling by public transport

And underneath, three column headings:

Dangers   Difficulties   Delights

Ask the class to contribute ideas for each column, for instance:

Dangers
– *risk of being mugged*
– *possibility of being hijacked*
– *overcrowding (on a ferry, for example), danger of capsizing*
– *no way out, in case of fire*

Difficulties
– *no place to stand/sit/lie down*
– *unpleasant smells of food*
– *filthy toilets*
– *incorrect information on display (about arrival/departure times, for instance)*
– *tedious travelling companions who talk too much or too little*

Delights
– *freedom from responsibility: when you travel, you do not have to work*
– *interest: constantly changing landscape*
– *opportunity of meeting interesting people*
– *being incognito: nobody knows who you are, or where you are going, and why*

2 Ask the students to form groups of four. Each group should draw up a ten-point plan for improvements which could be made to the public transport system of their own country (road, rail, sea, and air). Each suggestion should be as specific as possible: a comment such as 'improve ticket distribution' should be clarified by adding, for instance: 'We should be able to buy train tickets from all travel agencies, and not just from the main railway station.'

3 The groups compare and discuss their various suggestions.

(Optional) While the students are discussing, circulate to the groups copies of the sample texts. They should look for any points mentioned in the texts which would add fuel to their discussion, for example: 'The Metropolitan Police is often called upon to help transport officers in trouble; they suffer a much higher proportion of attacks than in other forces. This has mainly been because they are often unable to summon assistance since their radios do not communicate below surface and are useless on deep lines.'

SAMPLE TEXTS A

1 Memory

One had a lovely face,
And two or three had charm,
But charm and face were in vain
Because the mountain grass
Cannot but keep the form
Where the mountain hare has lain.

2 Goldfish

the scene of the crime
was a goldfish bowl
goldfish were kept
in the bowl at the time:
that was the scene
and that was the crime.

3 The Mosquito

The mosquito knows full well, small as he is
he's a beast of prey.
But after all
he only takes his bellyfull,
he doesn't put my blood in the bank.

4 Widowhood

She's over it by now, they say.
How can they tell?
She's over it by now.
And doing well.
Though I am still frozen,
And thawing is hell,
She's over it by now, they say,
And doing well.

5 Fire-love

Place two logs
close together
slightly apart –
each will eat out
the other's heart.

6 This Subway Station

This subway station
with its electric lights, pillars of steel,
arches of cement, and trains –
quite an improvement on the caves of the cavemen;
but, look! on this wall
a primitive drawing.

IN TIME OF
'THE BREAKING OF NATIONS'

Thomas Hardy
1840–1928

'Thou art my battle axe and weapons of war:
for with thee will I break in pieces the nations, and
with thee will I destroy kingdoms' (Jeremiah 51.20)

Only a man harrowing clods
   In a slow silent walk
With an old horse that stumbles and nods
   Half asleep as they stalk.

Only thin smoke without flame
   From the heaps of couch-grass;
Yet this will go onward the same
   Though Dynasties pass.

Yonder a maid and her wight
   Come whispering by:
War's annals will cloud into night
   Ere their story die.

Poems on the Underground

Faber · The British Library (Zweig Programme) · The British Council · Queen Mary College
Designed by MPD, LCP · typeset by APT 01-701 0477 · printed by First Impression 01-733 1182

SAMPLE TEXTS B

New Yorkers say some terrible things about the subway – that they hate it, or are scared stiff of it, or that it deserves to go broke. For tourists, it seems just another dangerous aspect of New York, though most don't know it exists. 'I haven't been down there in years,' is a common enough remark from a city dweller. Even people who ride it seem to agree that there is more Original Sin among subway passengers. And more desperation, too, making you think of choruses of 'O dark dark dark. They all go into the dark . . .'

'Subway' is not its name because, strictly-speaking, more than half of it is elevated. But which person who has ridden it lately is going to call it by its right name, 'The Rapid Transit'? It is also frightful-looking. It has paint and signatures all over its aged face. The graffiti is bad, violent and destructive, and is so extensive and so dreadful it is hard to believe that the perpetrators are not the recipients of some enormous foundation grant. The subway has been vandalized from end to end. It smells so hideous you want to put a clothes-pin on your nose, and it is so noisy the sound actually hurts. Is it dangerous? Ask anyone and he or she will tell you there are about two murders a day on the subway. It really is the pits, people say.

You have to ride it for a while to find out what it is and who takes it and who gets killed on it.

It is full of surprises. Three and a half million fares a day pass through it, and in the first nine months of last year the total number of murder victims on the subway amounted to six. This half-dozen does not include suicides (one a week), 'man-under' incident (one a day), or 'space-cases' – people who get themselves jammed between the train and the platform. Certainly the subway is very ugly and extremly noisy, but it only *looks* like a death-trap. People ride it looking stunned and holding their breath. It's not at all like the BART system in San Francisco, where people are constantly chattering, saying, 'I'm going to my father's wedding,' or 'I'm

looking after my mom's children,' or 'I've got a date with my
fiancée's boyfriend.' In New York, the subway is a serious matter –
the rackety train, the silent passengers, the occasional scream.

A lot of people say that. I did not believe it when he said it, and,
after a week of riding the trains, I still didn't. The subway is New
York City's best hope. The streets are impossible, the highways are
a failure, there is nowhere to park. The private automobile has no
future in this city whatsoever. This is plainest of all to the people
who own and use cars in the city; they know, better than anyone,
that the car is the last desperate old-fangled fling of a badly-planned
transport system. What is amazing is that back in 1904 a group of
businessmen solved New York's transport problems for centuries
to come. What vision! What enterprise! Whan an engineering
marvel they created in this underground railway! And how amazed
they would be to see what it has become, how foul-seeming to the
public mind.

When people say the subway frightens them, they are not being
silly or irrational. It is no good saying how cheap or how fast it is.
The subway *is* frightening. It is also very easy to get lost on the
subway, and the person who is lost in New York City has a serious
problem. New Yorkers make it their business to avoid getting lost.

It is the stranger who gets lost. It is the stranger who follows
people hurrying into the stair-well: subway entrances are just dark
holes in the sidewalk – the stations are below ground. There is
nearly always a bus-stop near the subway entrance. People waiting
at a bus-stop have a special pitying gaze for people entering the
subway. It is sometimes not pity, but fear, bewilderment, curiosity,
or fatalism; often they look like miners' wives watching their
menfolk going down the pit.

The stranger's sense of disorientation down below is immediate.
The station is all tile and iron and dampness; it has bars and
turnstiles and steel grates. It has the look of an old prison or a
monkey cage.

Buying a token, the stranger may ask directions, but the token
booth – reinforced, burglar-proof, bullet-proof – renders the reply
incoherent. And subway directions are a special language.

In any jungle, the pathway is a priority. People move around
New York in various ways, but the complexities of the subway have
allowed the New Yorker to think of his own route as something
personal, even *original*. No one uses maps on the subway – you
seldom see any. Most subway passengers were shown how to ride it
by parents or friends. Then habit turns it into instinct, just like a
trot down a jungle path. The passenger knows where he is going
because he never diverges from his usual route. But that is also
why, unless you are getting off at precisely his stop, he cannot tell
you how to get where you're going.

(Paul Theroux: 'Subterranean Gothic')

Crime and violence against Underground

Police plan new strategy to make the Tube safer

Terry Kirby, Crime Correspondent, reports that as London struggles to control crime on the Tube, Glasgow's system is almost crime-free.

MID-EVENING in the grimy booking hall of Manor House underground station on the Piccadilly line in north London: the escalators rumble in the background as a vagrant shuffles aimlessly in and out. Scruffy youngsters hang around the newspaper kiosk.

A middle-aged woman ticket inspector adopts a deliberately stern manner to deal with a smart young man who has tried to walk through without a ticket. After some discussion, he pays up.

While they were arguing, more young people walk past the kiosk, ignoring pleas from the collector inside.

This "one-woman-against-the-tide" tactic is the latest attempt by London Underground and British Transport Police to halt the crime wave on the system. While the ticket inspectors are the front line, the police are concealed as back-up.

Travellers who pay are in the clear but those who do not can be arrested for ticket fraud and be searched for weapons or other evidence of illegal activity.

The process is being repeated in two of the London areas showing alarmingly high increases in robberies: the northern ends of the Victoria and Piccadilly lines and the west London section of the Metropolitan line. The rise in robberies began in July last year and accelerated in 1988; figures for the whole system show an increase of 150 per cent in the first 10 weeks.

Supt Tony Stoppani of British Transport Police points out that the rise coincided with drives by the Metropolitan Police to tackle street crime; the muggers and pickpockets had been forced underground.

This is only part of a rise in all types of crime on the Underground - from 12,800 offences in 1980 to 17,000 in 1987.

Mr Stoppani is confident that crime can be "flushed out" with tactics like those at Manor House. "The Metropolitan Police are aware of the result of their policies. They realise that our problem is their problem too. What we have to try and do together is squeeze the criminal out." Where they will go he does not say.

There has to be a close relationship between the two forces. The Metropolitan Police is often called upon to help transport police officers in trouble; they suffer a much higher proportion of attacks than in other forces. This has mainly been because they are often unable to summon assistance since their radios do not communicate below surface and are useless on deep lines.

That is changing as part of a £15m plan to implement the 50 recommendations of the Department of Transport's 1986 report on Underground crime, which first identified the seriousness of the problem. The first 42 new deep level radios will be issued this year, with more to come.

Mr Stoppani considers this the single most effective means of improving police responses. "Our officers have to patrol in pairs for their own protection because they cannot easily summon help. With new radios they can patrol singly, knowing help is quickly at hand. This virtually doubles our available strength."

Other measures include a plan to install passenger alarms in vulnerable areas, linked to glass-enclosed "focal points" in concourses, where staff would supervise "safe" waiting areas. Nervous passengers would be told when trains are approaching their desired platforms; the focal points will be equipped with closed circuit television.

This is due to be implemented first at Oxford Circus, a haven for pickpockets, some stations at the south London end of the Northern line around Clapham, and on the northern extremity of the Central line.

Mr Stoppani concedes that monitor cameras have not been used well; there are many around the system but their introduction has been ad hoc and their purpose mainly operational. It will not be until a new central control room opens this year that there will begin to be feedback to police from existing and new cameras. The present control room is as shabby and cramped as some of the Northern line stations.

These efforts are in tandem with London Underground's costly refurbishment of stations: improving lighting, crowd control and introducing automatic ticket barriers. But, unlike Glasgow underground, it has not put staff in glass-fronted kiosks where they can view what is happening, but have mostly rebuilt the old-style offices where it is difficult to see in or out.

The prospects for the future are mixed. There have been some successes. CID squads formed to deal with robberies have managed to slow the rate of increase in the past few weeks and a concentration of efforts in the notorious Clapham and Stockwell area has resulted in a 20 per cent decrease in robberies since 1986.

Graffiti, costing £1m a year to remove, is getting worse and the policy of not allowing trains out with graffiti has been abandoned. Greater security at some depots and sidings has moved the vandals to other locations.

One ominous trend is in the youth of some offenders. "In recent months what has been very noticeable is the staggering increase in the involvement of children as young as 12 and 13. One 14-year-old is in custody over some very serious offences, while a number of accomplices have been identified – all around the same age," Mr Stoppani said.

A Tube driver trapped a gang of "steamers" robbing passengers on his train by pulling up his train short of a station and telling his line controller to call the police.

The driver, who has not been named, stopped the District line train outside South Kensington station late on Monday night to prevent the gang escaping after a passenger told him what was happening.

The gang had boarded the train at Victoria and were running through the carriages grabbing money and jewellery from other passengers. The driver awaited the arrival of British Transport Police officers who arrested seven juveniles.

(*The Independent*, 6 April 1988)

How Big Brother keeps trouble off the Clockwork Orange

A YOUNG boy being led away from a station by his mother was brandishing a large knife with a serrated blade. It was plastic, but realistic.

"That is about the closest you will get to violence here," said Bob Adams, manager of the Glasgow Underground - nicknamed the "Clockwork Orange" because of its orange-painted trains, rather than a violent reputation.

Mr Adams searched his files for anything worse than youths sliding down escalator handrails. He finds it: "We had some football supporters who leapt the ticket barriers without paying and went onto the platform.

"We spotted them on the screens and used the public address system to tell them to go back and pay immediately. And they did."

Mr Adams pointed out that the supporters were not from Glasgow. Local fans knew better, he said. "They pay; they know the procedure and know it isn't worth it."

Recognising that the system is under tight control and that any misdemeanour is likely to be swiftly spotted appears to be crucial to the success of the Underground system in remaining almost completely crime-free.

Comparisons with London are difficult. Glasgow Underground is far smaller and although Victorian in origin, was totally rebuilt in the late 1970s to help regenerate the inner city.

As a 15-station, flat fare, one-line system having only one interchange with the overground railway, it lacks the dark passageways and corners of the London system. The kind of atmosphere which encourages disrespect does not exist.

Each station has only one central platform or two side platforms. The trains are clean and regular. The system is well used and at 14 million passenger journeys a year is close to capacity.

Despite Glasgow's reputation as a tough city, crime was never a serious problem on the underground even before it was rebuilt when it was as dingy as many central London stations are now. The system was always relatively graffiti-free. The rebuilding provided an opportunity to ensure crime did not take a hold.

Most stations have a light, open atmosphere and are constructed with a mixture of ceramic tiles, smooth bricks and perspex that is difficult to vandalise and easy to clean.

The ticket offices are glass bubbles, so staff can see and be seen - designed on the basis that uniforms discourage misbehaviour. Vagrants are kept out and passengers are kept under watch.

Monitor cameras are placed in the larger station halls and at both ends of every platform. Pictures are relayed to their own station offices and to the control room at Govan where the controllers can play Big Brother.

"Nobody gets up to anything because they know we are watching them," said duty controller Douglas McPherson. "I can talk to and see almost every part of the system at the flick of a switch. If you tell them to stop, they usually do." He cannot see inside the carriages of the trains but can talk to the passengers through the drivers. The ticket offices are also alarm-linked to him.

The biggest control problem is football supporters - Ibrox station has an entrance used only for Rangers matches - and a senior police officer is present in the control room linked to officers on the streets to ensure co-ordination.

At other times, police are summoned by the controller using 999 calls - there is no need to have a direct control room to control room link.

Strathclyde Police has a visible presence because officers are encouraged to use the system during normal work and beat officers associate themselves with the stations on their patch. Otherwise, the police have no special officer or team involved in the underground and do not even collate figures for underground crime as a separate category.

(*The Independent*, 6 April 1988)

4 Over to you: further ideas, with a focus on language

Introduction

In the first three sections of this book, we have concentrated mainly on approaches to literature. That is, on different ways in which literary texts can be used to generate discussion.

Here, in the final section, we suggest some of the ways in which these approaches can be adapted to focus more closely on language.

Clearly it is not possible to cover all the areas of language which could usefully be practised through literary texts. What we are offering here are suggestions for further development. These are ideas to begin with. After that – over to you.

Some general points

In searching for material, much time can be saved if you decide in advance precisely what you are looking for. Is it, for instance, the use of the passive? conditional forms? articles? -*ing* forms, phrasal and prepositional verbs?

Once you have decided what the language focus should be, and have selected your material, check through the following questions:

a. Do the texts illustrate a variety of uses of the selected language structure or item (different uses of the words *got* or *go*, or different structures following the word *if*)?

b. Does the language of the text(s) reflect natural usage, or is it exceptional? (Sample texts should, as far as possible, reflect customary usage.)

c. Is the context clear? Can the students interpret the language correctly without needing further information?

d. How useful are the passages? Will the students learn anything new by working on them? Or are the texts merely being used to illustrate points of grammar?

e. Could the use of language in the literary texts be contrasted with the use of similar structures or expressions in non-literary texts?

About the activities

The section begins with activities which focus on three very different areas of language: vocabulary, tenses, and conditional forms.

In 4.1 *Focus on language: vocabulary*, the emphasis is on passive understanding. The words selected for discussion are ones which the students should be able to recognize and understand in reading, but not necessarily to use. This helps to counterbalance the emphasis on the active use of language in earlier activities (as in 2.7 *Suggesting the words*.

In 4.2 *Focus on language: tenses* and 4.3 *Focus on language: conditional forms*, the focus is on structure rather than vocabulary. Many other comparable areas of language could be explored in the same way (the future tense, *-ing* forms, and modals such as *may, might, must, could, should, would*).

Activities 4.4 and 4.5 *Translation* open up endless possibilities, particularly in the exploration of colloquial and formal language and the use of idiomatic expressions. In the two activities outlined here, we have tried to show how translation can be used to sharpen the students' sensitivity to everyday language. The section ends with activities designed to develop listening and writing skills through literature.

4.1 Focus on language: vocabulary

LEVEL

Lower intermediate to advanced

TIME

15 – 20 minutes

PREPARATION

Select a text (prose or poetry) which you feel would help to expand the students' passive vocabulary, and make it up into a task sheet. Remove certain of the words, and for each blank space offer three alternatives, one of which should be the word actually used in the text. In our sample task sheet, for instance, the activity looks like this:

Task sheet A
The word 'tourist' seems naturally to suggest haste and (1) . . .
1 a) compulsion   b) impatience   c) mindlessness
(The word actually used was *compulsion*.)

Task sheet B
Ladies (3) . . . like birds with their bright and pointed feet,
3 a) tiptoeing   b) strutting   c) stepping
(The word actually used was *stepping*.)

IN CLASS

1 Give each of the students a copy of your task sheet. Ask the students to work on their own, and to select the alternatives they consider most appropriate for the blank spaces.

2 After five to eight minutes, the students form groups of four and discuss their choices. After the discussion, reveal the original wording to the class.

NOTES

1 The advantage of this technique is that you can select the texts to suit your students' language level. Of the two sample texts given, the prose passage (task sheet A) would be most suitable for advanced students, while the poem (task sheet B) could be used from intermediate level upwards.

2 It is important to remember that this is not a multiple choice exercise, and that the alternatives given are not meant to be distractors. Each of the alternatives should be possible in context. The function of the alternatives is to encourage the students to consider the differences between the three words, and to think more carefully about the author's choice.

3 This approach is a useful way both of refreshing familiar texts and of introducing new ones.

TASK SHEET A

Read through the text below and consider the alternatives a), b), and c) given for each blank. Select the one you consider most suitable in each case.

The word 'tourist' seems naturally to suggest haste and (1) . . . . One thinks of those pitiable droves of Middle West school teachers whom one encounters suddenly at street corners and in public buildings, (2) . . ., breathless, their heads singing with unfamiliar names, their bodies strained and bruised from scrambling in and out of motor charabancs, up and down staircases, and from trailing (3) . . . through miles of gallery and museum at the heels of a facetious and (4) . . . guide. How their eyes haunt us long after they have passed on to the next phase of their itinerary – haggard and uncomprehending eyes, mildly (5) . . ., like those of animals in pain, eloquent of that world-weariness we all feel at the dead weight of European culture. Must they go on to the very end? Is there no (6) . . . in this pitiless rite? Must reverence still be done to the past? As each peak of their climb is (7) . . . scaled, each monument on the schedule ticked off as seen, the horizon recedes farther before them. And as one sits at one's café table and sees them stumble by, one sheds not wholly (8) . . . tears for these poor scraps of humanity thus trapped and mangled in the machinery of uplift.

(Evelyn Waugh: *Labels*)

1 a) compulsion   b) impatience   c) mindlessness
2 a) bemused   b) baffled   c) bewildered
3 a) wearily   b) abjectly   c) disconsolately
4 a) disdainful   b) haughty   c) contemptuous
5 a) resentful   b) accusing   c) reproachful
6 a) respite   b) remission   c) relief
7 a) doggedly   b) resolutely   c) laboriously
8 a) mocking   b) derisive   c) scornful

KEY TO TASK

Original wording:

1 a	3 c	5 a	7 c
2 b	4 c	6 a	8 b

TASK SHEET B

Read through the poem below and consider the alternatives a), b), and c) given for each blank. Select the one you consider most suitable in each case.

After the Opera

Down the stone stairs
Girls with their large eyes (1) . . . with tragedy
Lift looks of shocked and (2) . . . emotion up at me.
And I smile.

Ladies
(3) . . . like birds with their bright and pointed feet
(4) . . . anxiously forth, as if for a boat to carry them out of the wreckage;
And among the wreck of the theatre crowd
I stand and smile.
They take tragedy so (5) . . .;
Which pleases me.

But when I meet the (6) . . . eyes
The reddened, (7) . . . eyes of the barman with thin arms
I am glad (8) . . . .

(D. H. Lawrence 'After the Opera')

1 a) wide	b) tear-stained	c) fraught	
2 a) grand	b) momentous	c) passionate	
3 a) Walking	b) Stepping	c) Strutting	
4 a) Glance	b) Gaze	c) Peer	
5 a) much to heart	b) personally	c) becomingly	
6 a) tired	b) weary	c) exhausted	
7 a) pained	b) aching	c) raw	
8 a) to leave	b) to get away	c) to go back to where I came from	

KEY TO TASK

Original wording:

1 a	3 b	5 c	7 b
2 b	4 c	6 b	8 c

4.2 Focus on language: tenses

LEVEL

Lower intermediate to advanced

TIME

10 – 15 minutes

PREPARATION

1 Select a passage which can easily be understood out of context, and which contains a range of different tenses.

2 Remove some of the verbs or verbal phrases from the text, and replace them with the infinitive form of the verb in brackets, as in this example from our task sheet:

As he (1 *go*) home, just as he (2 *pass*) the Bargello, he stopped. He put his hand to his breast pocket. He (3 *rob*).
Key: (1 *was going*), (2 *was passing*), (3 *had been robbed*)

3 Make up your task sheet and provide enough copies for the whole class.

IN CLASS

1 Give each student a copy of the task sheet. Allow five to seven minutes for the students to note down their suggestions for the appropriate tenses.

2 *Class discussion.* Ask the students to call out their suggestions for each of the verbs in brackets. After listening to the various suggestions, reveal the original wording.

NOTES

1 In some respects, this approach is no different from the standard textbook exercise: 'Put the verbs in the following sentences into the correct tense.' There is, however, one important difference. In the standard approach, the students work on model (or 'made up') sentences which have no real context. Here, by contrast, they work on a coherent passage which not only provides a clear context, but also makes it easier for the students to decide which form of the verb is most suitable.

2 Many other features of language such as the different uses of contracted and full forms (*I've/I have*), use of the passive, articles, prepositions, and so on can be explored through literature in a similar way.

3 See also 2.7 *Suggesting the words.*

<u>TASK SHEET</u>   Read the passage below and note down the correct tense of the verb
                          in brackets.

Aaron found himself in the street. It was half-past seven. The night
was fine now. He had his overcoat over his arm.

Leaving the Piazza, a gang of soldiers suddenly (1 *rush*) round
him, buffeting him in one direction, whilst another gang, swinging
round the corner, (2 *throw*) him back helpless again into the midst
of the first gang. For some moments he struggled among the rude,
brutal little mob of grey-green uniforms that (3 *smell*) so strong of
soldiers. Then, irritated, he (4 *find*) himself free again.

As he (5 *go*) home, suddenly, just as he (6 *pass*) the Bargello, he
stopped, and put his hand to his breast-pocket. His letter-case was
gone. He (7 *rob*). It was as if lightning (8 *run*) through him at that
moment. For a moment, unconscious and superconscious, he (9
stand) there. They had put their hand in his breast and robbed him.
If they (10 *stab*) him it could hardly have had a greater effect on
him.

Feeling quite weak and faint, he walked on. And as soon as he
began to walk, he began to reason. Perhaps his letter-case (11 *be*) in
his other coat. Perhaps the (12 *not have*) it with him at all.

He hurried forward. He wanted to make sure. He wanted relief
. . . Reaching the house, he hastened upwards to his lonely room.
He shut the door and switched on the light. Then he searched his
other pockets. He looked everywhere. In vain. For he *knew* the
thing was stolen. He (13 *know*) it all along. The soldiers deliberately
(14 *plot*). The must (15 *watch*) him previously. He sat down in a
chair, to recover from the shock. The pocket-book contained four
hundred francs, three one-pound notes, and various letters. Well,
these were lost.

And now he sat, weak in every limb, and said to himself: 'Yes –
and if I (16 *not rush along*) so full of feeling, it would (17 *never
happen*). I gave myself away. It is my own fault. I should (18 *be on
my guard*). I should always be on my guard.

So he rose and tidied himself for dinner. His face was now set,
and still. His heart was also still – and fearless.

(D. H. Lawrence: *Aaron's Rod* (abridged))

<u>KEY TO TASK</u>   Original wording:

1 rushed	10 had stabbed
2 threw	11 was
3 smelt	12 had not had
4 found	13 had known
5 was going	14 had (deliberately) plotted
6 was passing	15 have watched
7 had been robbed	16 hadn't rushed
8 ran	17 never have happened
9 stood	18 have been on my guard

4.3 Focus on language: conditional forms and *if*-clauses

LEVEL Intermediate to advanced

TIME Flexible

PREPARATION 1 For this activity you will need a text which illustrates the use in English of conditional words such as *if, would, could, were,* and *had.* Look through your text and remove some parts of the conditional structures (such as those in italics in the example below):

Rita You wouldn't leave her. Not when she's like this.
Jean I would if *I had a good enough excuse.*
Rita Well, why don't you just go? That's all the excuse you need.
Jean *Would you* stay with her if I did?
Rita I'd stay till Mel got back.

2 Make a copy of the text, leaving gaps for the structures you have chosen. Mark each gap with a number and, on a separate sheet, draw up a list of the missing expressions.

3 Make enough copies of the text for one third of the class.

IN CLASS 1 Ask the students to work in groups of three. Give each group a copy of the text. Each group should discuss possible wordings for the blank spaces.

2 The groups compare their ideas.

3 *Class discussion.* Ask the class to suggest words to fill the gaps in the text. After listening to the various suggestions, and commenting (where necessary) on points of language, reveal the original wording.

NOTES You may, perhaps, feel that it is not fair to use literature merely as material for illustrating points of language which could equally well be practised through non-fictional texts. Such reservations are quite understandable, since it is commonly accepted that literature is studied primarily for content rather than for structure. However, we would suggest that:

a. Literature is just as suitable for language study as is any other form of written material. And in certain respects, in the use of the spoken language, for example, literature is even more suitable because it creates a real, but unpredictable context. (Many textbook contexts are, by contrast, unreal and predictable.)

b. If we focus on the language of literature, this does not mean that we are ignoring the meaning. Far from it. In order to predict a structure or expression, we need to be attuned to the whole text. To take an example from the sample text in the task sheet:

Rita What keeps you here?
Jean I don't know.

Rita You wouldn't (1) . . . Now when she's like this.
Jean I would if (2) . . .
Rita Well, why don't you just go? That's all the excuse you need.

Here, the students are asked to suggest what might have been said in the gaps. In each case, a clue is given in what is said later. There is a logical link between Rita's first remark: 'You wouldn't (*leave her*)', and her second: 'Well, *why don't you just go?*' And, similarly, between Jean's words: 'I would if (*I had a good enough excuse*)', and Rita's response: 'That's all the excuse you need.'

Literature can help to correct errors in the students' use of language. In this particular activity, one of the common errors which could be corrected is the tendency of non-native speakers to use full forms of the conditional ('I do not love Mother and yet I am stuck with her,' or 'You would have loved her more if she had left the house between us.') instead of the more natural short forms ('I don't love Mother and yet I'm stuck with her,' 'You'd've loved her more if she'd left the house between us.')

TASK SHEET

Read the dialogue below and discuss with your partners what words you feel would be most suitable in the gaps.

(Rita and Jean are sisters. Jean is at present living in the house of their mother, who is dying. Although Rita has children to support (and no money) it is Jean who will inherit the house. During the conversation, Rita suggests, amongst other things, that Jean is not happily married to her husband, Mel.)

Jean Are you glad you've got children?
Rita Of course I am.
Jean No. I mean really. When you think about it.
Rita Yes. I am glad when I think about it.
Jean Why?
Rita I love them.
Jean What good does that do you?
Rita It's better to love people, isn't it?
Jean I don't know.
Rita It doesn't make sense otherwise.
Jean It doesn't make sense anyway. I don't love Mother and yet I'm stuck with her.
Rita You do love her.
Jean I'm sick of her.
Rita Why are you here then? What keeps you here?
Jean I don't know.
Rita You wouldn't (1) . . . . Not when she's like this.
Jean I would if (2) . . .
Rita Well, why don't you just go? That's all the excuse you need.
Jean (3) . . . stay with her if I did?
Rita I'd stay till Mel got back.
Jean He wouldn't do anything. What would you do if he (4) . . .?

Rita Well, I couldn't stay indefinitely. I'd have to (5) . . . some time.
Jean How long would you stay?
Rita I don't know. I'd try and stay till she died.
Jean What if she (6) . . .?
Rita Oh, I don't know. I'd (7) . . . . I don't know. It's different when you've got children.
Jean God.
Rita Look, Jean, you can feel sorry for yourself all you like but don't expect me to. You wanted to live in this house. You and Mel could've (8) . . . years ago. There was no need for you to stay here. Mother didn't need you then.
Jean She never wanted me to leave. And anyway, it would've been (9) . . . on her own. Living by yourself's no joke.
Rita You only stayed for what you could get. A house this size is worth a fortune. Ted and I are struggling. A lot of his money goes to the other kids. And what'll we get when she dies? Half of whatever's left in the bank. That's all. You'll waltz off with the other half. If I was you, Jean, I'd (10) . . . . You're all set to make a financial killing within the next few days.
  (Mother's eyes closed)
Jean You'd've loved her more if she'd (11) . . ., wouldn't you?
Rita Yes, I would've appreciated it. I would've seen some sense in it. It would've been (12) . . . . I've got children.

(Catherine Hayes: *Skirmishes*)

KEY TO TASK   Original wording of the text:

1 leave her	7 put her in a home
2 I had a good enough excuse	8 bought a place of your own
3 would you	9 lonely for her
4 didn't come back	10 stay put
5 go home	11 left the house between us
6 started to get better	12 fair

4.4 Translation 1: dialogue

LEVEL   Intermediate

TIME   25 – 30 minutes

PREPARATION   1 Choose a passage, preferably one containing dialogue, from a novel, short story, or play. If the context is not immediately clear, give a short summary of the situation, or add the preceding paragraph in brackets. (The text in brackets need not be translated.)

2 Select any language features of the text to which you wish to draw the students' attention. Mark the relevant words either by underlining them in the text or by providing guideline notes, such as those given after the task sheet.

IN CLASS

1 Ask the students to form groups of three. Give each group a copy of the full text, but ask them to translate only one-third of it (on the sample task sheet, lines 1–14, 15–28, 29–42). Make sure that at least two groups are working on the same section of text.

2 After fifteen minutes, ask each group to compare translations with another group which has worked on the same section of text.

3 *Class discussion.* Which lines were most difficult to translate? What were the best translations suggested? Was there anything that could not be adequately translated?

NOTES

1 In selecting material for this activity, we suggest that you look for passages which are easy to understand and which, as far as possible, reflect the everyday use of language. Hence the emphasis on dialogue.

If translation is to be used effectively in the language class, it should be an activity which is free from anxiety and open to discussion. Students should not be asked (as they often are) to translate obscure and unnecessarily complex passages of prose. And the texts chosen should provide interesting challenges, not insurmountable problems.

2 Many of the passages in this book would be suitable for translation, particularly those in 2.2 *Speculation 2*, and 2.7 *Suggesting the words*.

3 See, also in this series, Alan Duff: *Translation*, for ideas on using translation to reinforce specific points of language.

TASK SHEET

Translate the dialogue below, paying particular attention to the phrases in the notes that follow.

(At the beginning of the novel *The French Lieutenant's Woman*, Charles and Ernestina, who are planning to marry, are walking along a steep path by the seaside. Ernestina is leading the way.)

'Now, am I not kind to bring you here? And look.' (She led him to the side of the rampart, where a line of flat stones inserted sideways into the wall served as rough steps down to a lower walk. 'These are the very steps that Jane Austen made Louisa
5   Musgrove fall down in *Persuasion*.')
'How romantic.'
'Gentlemen were romantic . . . then.'
'And are scientific now? Shall we make the perilous descent?'
10   'On the way back.'

(Once again they walked on. It was only then that he noticed, or at least realized the sex of, the figure at the end.)

'Good heavens, I took that to be a fisherman. But isn't it a woman?'

15 Ernestina peered – her grey, very pretty eyes, were short-sighted, and all she could see was a dark shape.

'Is she young?'

'It's too far to tell.'

'But I can guess who it is. It must be poor Tragedy.'

20 'Tragedy?'

'A nickname. One of her nicknames.'

'And what are the others?'

'The fishermen have a gross name for her.'

'My dear Tina, you can surely . . .'

25 'They call her the French Lieutenant's . . . Woman.'

'Indeed. And is she so ostracized that she has to spend her days out here?'

'She is . . . a little mad. Let us turn. I don't like to go near her.'

They stopped. He stared at the black figure.

30 'But I'm intrigued. Who is this French Lieutenant?'

'A man she is said to have . . .'

'Fallen in love with?'

'Worse than that.'

'And he abandoned her? There is a child?'

35 No. I think no child. It is all gossip.'

'But what is she doing there?'

'They say she waits for him to return.'

'But . . . does no one care for her?'

'She is a servant of some kind to old Mrs Poulteney. She is

40 never to be seen when we visit. But she lives there. Please let us turn back. I did not see her.'

(John Fowles: *The French Lieutenant's Woman*)

Notes

line 7   *Gentlemen were romantic then.* The word *then* must suggest time past (the 18th century). Could the translation of *then* come at the beginning of the sentence?

line 8   *And are scientific now?* Would a synonym be more suitable in translation, say, *practical, rational*?
          Shall we make the perilous descent? Would it be the same if Charles said: *Shall we go down the steep way?* Is he joking, or trying to give her courage?

line 13   *I took that to be a fisherman.* What is the most suitable translation for: *I took that to be . . .?* Can a link be made between *that* and *it* (isn't *it* a woman? *line 13*)?

line 18   *It's too far to tell.* Possibilities for rewording (in translation): *You/one can't tell from this distance/I can't see from here/We're too far away to see.*

line 23 . . . *a gross name for her.* What does *gross* mean? *Vulgar, ugly, common, rude?* Is the dictionary definition suitable?

line 24 . . . *you can surely* . . . If Charles had continued, what would he have said? Perhaps: *You can surely not mean to suggest that she is (a loose woman)?* The translation should suggest a similar uncompleted construction.

line 26 Indeed. How does Charles say this word – with astonishment, or no great surprise?

. . . *is she so ostracized* . . . It may be necessary in translation to change the structure, and use an active form: *Everyone openly condemns her.*

line 31 A man she is said to have . . . Make sure that the structure of this sentence (in translation) fits in with the next line: . . . *fallen in love with.*

line 34 There is a child? Is this a statement, a question, or both? Why does Charles put in this way, instead of asking, for instance: *Does she have a child?/Do they have a child?*, or *Because of a child?*

line 35 It is all gossip. Do not be too much influenced by the English structure.

line 38 But . . . *does no one care for her?* Does this mean: *Does no one like her?*, or *Does no one look after her?* or both?

line 40 She is never to be seen . . . Does this mean: *We can never see her when we visit* or *When we visit, we never see her?*

4.5 Translation 2: everyday words

LEVEL

Lower intermediate upwards

TIME

20 – 30 minutes

PREPARATION

1 The purpose of this activity is to explore the different ways in which everyday words such as *get, go, give, have, put, take,* are used in English.

2 Make a selection of seven to ten short passages. Once you have decided which words and expressions you wish to concentrate on, underline them in the text. In looking for suitable material, bear in mind the following points:

a. The passages should be self-explanatory, that is, the students should be able to work on them without needing to know more about the context.

b. The passages should illustrate a range of different usages of the chosen word or expression in English (literal, formal/informal, idiomatic), as in this excerpt from sample text 6:

'*Got* a new boy friend?'

'I've *got* to see a man on business.'

'Have you *got* a job there?'

'I'm probably going to *get* a car soon.'

c. The material should offer a challenge to the students. That is, it should encourage them to use a variety of expressions when translating into their own language.

3 Make enough copies of your set of passages for one third of the class.

4 Below, we describe how the sample texts, which focus on the words *go* and *get*, could be used in class.

IN CLASS

1 Ask the students to work in groups of three. Give each group approximately half of the texts you have chosen (1–5, or 6–8). Ask the students to decide how they would translate the expressions in italics. The remainder of the text can be translated orally.

2 Each group compares its suggestions with another group which has worked on the same set of texts.

3 The groups exchange texts. (Those who have worked on passages 1–5 exchange with those who have worked on passages 6–8). Again, they translate the expressions in italics, and compare their suggestions with another group.

4 *Class discussion.* Which expressions were most difficult to translate? Which were easiest, and why?

NOTES

1 We have concentrated here on just one tiny part of language: the words *go* and *get*, and the expressions associated with them. This may seem like a minimalist approach. But it is not. By working on these few examples, the students will not only be exploring some of the meanings of *go* and *get*, but also reflecting, in two languages, on broader questions such as word order, emphasis, register, style, and meaning.

2 Many other activities in this book could also be adapted for translation. We would suggest in particular, 2.7 *Suggesting the words*, and 4.3 *Focus on language*.

SAMPLE TEXTS

1 (The scene takes place in court, during a murder trial.)

'After it was all over, what did you do?'
'I went home.'
'A serious and terrible crime had been committed *and you went home*, tucked yourself up in bed *and went to sleep*! . . . When you went to bed, *did you go alone?*'
'*I don't see what that's got to do with it.*' Her answer had a hint of sharpness.
'Did you go alone?'

'I told you. *I went to bed.*'
'Miss Evans. I shall ask my question again *and I shall go on asking it all night* if it's necessary in the interests of my client . . . Did you go to bed alone?'
'Yes. I went to bed alone.'
'*How long had that been going on?*'
'How long had what been going on, Mr Rumpole?' Sam (the judge) asked.
'That the witness had taken to sleeping alone, my Lord.'

(John Mortimer: *Rumpole of the Bailey*)

2 The only playwright I knew was Sean O'Casey. His room was bare and contained only an iron bed, a table, and a couple of poor chairs. On the shabby wall was a notice he had printed:

> GET ON WITH THE BLOODY PLAY

(V. S. Pritchett: *Midnight Oil*)

3 The narrator is walking in Italy, wearing tight shoes.)

I had a terrific pain in the ankle, so *by the time I got to* Piacenza railway station I had *barely enough strength left to get my wallet out.*

(Clive James: *Unreliable Memoirs*)

4 'Betty, you can't do it,' he said. 'It's simply out of the question.'
'Why?'
'He's awful.'
'I don't think he is. I think he's rather nice.'
'*Are you going to pretend you're in love with him?*'
'I think it would be tactful, don't you?'
'*Why are you going to marry him?*'
She looked at him coolly.
'He's got pots of money. I'm nearly twenty-six.'

(Somerset Maugham: *The Human Element*)

5 Mrs Simon's small face tightened, hardened, went a shade whiter among the pillows. Her manner became a positive invitation to Mrs Bettersley to go away.
   Mrs Bettersley, moving to the edge of the bed, caught the girl's wrists and firmly, but not untenderly, forced them apart.
'*We've got three-quarters of an hour alone,*' she said. '*You've got to tell me. Make it come into words.* When it's once out, it won't hurt – like a tooth, you know.'

(Elizabeth Bowen: 'The Apple Tree')

6 Sally shrugged her shoulders with a slight, impatient, listless movement. Throughout this conversation, I noticed that she avoided my eyes. I began to wonder how soon I could *make an excuse to go.*

Then the telephone bell rang. Sally yawned, pulled the
instrument across on to her lap. (. . .) 'And now, darling, I must
fly!' cried Sally, when, at last, the conversation was over. 'I'm
about two hours late already!'
'*Got a new boy friend?*'
But Sally ignored my grin.
'*I've got to see a man on business,*' she said briefly.
'And when shall we meet again?'
'I'll have to see, darling . . . *I've got such a lot on*, just at present
. . . I'll let you know . . . *I may be going to Frankfurt quite soon.*'
'*Have you got a job there?*'
'No. Not exactly.' Sally's voice was brief, dismissing this subject.
(. . .)
We walked out together to the corner of the street, where Sally
picked up a taxi.
'It's an awful nuisance living so far off,' she said. '*I'm probably
going to get a car soon.* Well, goodbye, darling. I'll see you
sometime.'
'Goodbye, Sally. Enjoy yourself.'

(Christopher Isherwood: *Goodbye to Berlin*)

7 'Anyway,' she added a moment later, 'I know *I've got a
temperature*; my eyes hurt when I move them.'
'*Better get the doctor then.*'
'You don't sound very sympathetic, I must say.'
'*I've got a train to catch*, as you perfectly well know.'
She wanted to say, 'You didn't have a train to catch yesterday,'
but hesitated.
'Be sure to call me at the office if you're feeling really bad.'
He was getting late, and his hangover had by no means subsided.

(Elizabeth Jane Howard: *Odd Girl Out*)

8 'Do you want money? I'll give it to you if you like! . . . I'll give
you two hundred marks if you'll kiss me.'
'What a condition! And I don't want to kiss you – I don't like
kissing. *Please go!*'
'Yes – you do! – yes, you do.' He caught hold of her arms above
the elbows. She struggled, and was quite amazed to realize how
angry she felt.
'*Let me go* – immediately!' she cried . . . 'Leave me alone, I tell
you!'
'Well, *kiss me and I'll go.*'
'I won't kiss you! – you brute! – I won't!' Somehow she slipped
out of his arms and ran to the wall. '*Get out!*' she stammered. '*Go
on now*, clear out!' She thrilled at her own angry voice. 'To think
I should talk to a man like that!'
He made a rush at her, and held her against the wall. This time
she could not get free.

(Katherine Mansfield: 'The Swing of the Pendulum')

4.6 Listening: stress and pause

LEVEL

Lower intermediate upwards

TIME

15 – 20 minutes

PREPARATION

For this activity, you will need a recording of a dialogue passage from a play, novel, or short story.

Sources of suitable recorded material include:
– British Council libraries
– BBC World Service
– Public libraries
– Good Book Guides
– Recorded Book Services

1 Select a section of the dialogue (lasting about three minutes) in which the speakers frequently pause or give special stress to certain words.

2 Make copies of the text of the extract you have chosen for the students to listen to in class. There should be enough copies for each student to have his or her own.

IN CLASS

1 Make sure that you can easily find the passage you have chosen on the tape (note the number on the counter). Now, play the students about five minutes of the dialogue which comes before the passage you have chosen.

2 When you reach the chosen passage, stop the cassette recorder. Tell the students that you are going to give them copies of the text which comes after the passage they have just heard.

3 Give the students copies of the text. Ask them to work on their own for about five minutes. They should look through the dialogue and underline any words they think will be stressed by the speakers, or any words which will be spoken in a special tone (softly, angrily, sarcastically).

They should also mark with a V any places where they would expect the speakers to pause. The sample text shows how a text can be marked for stress and pause.

4 After about eight minutes, ask the students to form groups of three and to compare the pauses and stresses they have marked on their texts.

5 Play the recording to the class, and ask the students to compare their markings with the stresses and pauses actually used by the speakers. Allow the students to hear the recording at least twice.

NOTES

1 One of the main aims of this activity is to bring the printed page to life for the students. That is, through listening, to bring out important features of language such as stress and intonation, which may be lost in silent reading. What the eye misses, the ear may easily pick up: a note of irony, or perhaps evasiveness. For

instance:

'What do you think of her? Is she not very charming?
'Oh! yes – very – a very pleasing young woman.'
(Jane Austen)

'Well, how do you like Sydney?'
'The harbour, I think, is wonderful.'
(D. H. Lawrence)

2 You may need to remind the students that in this activity there
are no absolutely 'right' answers. No two readers will give exactly
the same interpretation of a text. The aim of asking the students to
predict how the text will be spoken is to encourage them to listen
more attentively to the way in which it *is* spoken.

SAMPLE TEXT

Frank What are you doing here? V It's <u>Thursday</u>, you . . .
Rita I know I shouldn't be here, it's me dinner hour, but listen,
I've gorra tell someone, V have you got a few minutes, can
y' spare . . .
Frank My God, what <u>is</u> it?
Rita I <u>had</u> to come an' tell y', Frank, last night V , I went to the
theatre! A proper one, a professional theatre.
Frank For God's sake, you had me worried V , I thought it was
something serious.
Rita No, listen, it <u>was</u>. I went out and got me ticket V , it was
Shakespeare, V I thought it was gonna be <u>dead borin'</u> . . .
Frank Then why did you go in the first place?
Rita I wanted to find out. V But listen, it <u>wasn't</u> borin', it was
bleedin' <u>great</u> . . .

4.7 Listening: selective recall

LEVEL Lower intermediate upwards

TIME 15 – 20 minutes

PREPARATION 1 As in activity 4.6, you will need a recording of a passage of
dialogue for this activity. The passage you choose should be about
ten minutes in length, and it should preferably contain dialogue
which is close to everyday speech. (A suitable text would be, for
instance, one similar to the extract from *Skirmishes* in 4.3 *Focus on
Language*.)

2 You will not need copies of the text for the students, but you
should have a copy for yourself to consult while playing the
recording.

3 Listen to the recording and mark any of the dialogue exchanges which you think the students would be able to recall at least partly, from memory. For example:

Jean Are you glad you've got children?
Rita Of course I am.
Jean No. I mean really. When you think about it.
Rita Yes. I am glad when I think about it.

IN CLASS

1 Play the recording of the passage you have chosen. When it is finished, ask the students to recall as much as they can of the situation:

– *Who were the speakers?*
– *Where were they?*
– *What various things did they talk about?*
– *Did either of them say anything unexpected or striking?*

2 Now play the recording again. But this time, stop the tape at certain chosen points (see *Preparation*) and ask the students to recall, as accurately as they can, the words which follow immediately after the pause.

3 Listen to all suggestions, and write up some of the best ones on the board. Then continue playing the tape, until you reach the next stopping-point. Then proceed with the recall, as before. Follow the same procedure through to the end of the tape.

4 Play the recording once again, right through, without a break.

NOTES

1 This activity has two important functions – to assist:

a. *Listening comprehension.* Did the students understand what they heard? Was there anything that escaped them, or that they misinterpreted?

b. *Reformulation.* In attempting to recall the words that were used, are the students able to find different, but equally acceptable ways of saying the same thing?

An important skill in language learning is the ability to reformulate, to say the same thing in different ways. This is why it is important to write up some of the students' suggestions on the board, as these will later serve as a useful point of comparison.

2 A useful follow-up to this activity would be 2.7 *Suggesting the words*.

4.8 Listening: What happens next?

LEVEL
Advanced

TIME
15 – 20 minutes

PREPARATION
1 Find a recording of a short passage of prose which leads up to a climax or resolution. A suitable passage in this book would be, for instance, the extract from *The Woman in White*, in 2.4 *Storylines 2*.

2 Choose a point towards the end of the recording at which you will stop – about one minute (or one page) from the end of the passage.

3 Make copies of the text which comes *after* the point at which you will stop the recording. You will need one copy for each group of three students.

IN CLASS
1 Explain to the students that you are going to play them a recording of an episode from a literary text (novel, play, or story), and that you will stop the recording shortly before the end.

2 Play the recording to the whole class, and stop at the point you have chosen.

3 Ask the students to form groups of three and to discuss how they think the episode ends. They should note down all details they think will be mentioned, including any remarks they expect the characters to make.

4 Allow ten minutes for discussion, then give each group a copy of the text of the missing part of the recording. They should look through the text to find any points which they predicted.

5 *Round-up discussion.* How close did the various groups come to the original text in their prediction of the ending?

6 Finally, play the end of the recording.

NOTES
Listening generally takes less time than silent reading (at least, in a foreign language). The advantage of this activity, then, is that it allows you to work with a fairly lengthy text without having to hurry the students on. The listening enables you to save time for the in-depth reading.

VARIATION
Ask your partner

PREPARATION
For this variation you will need fewer copies of the text – one copy for every six students in the class.

IN CLASS
1 An interesting variation, which will require some co-operation from the students, is to split the class into two equal groups. Give one group (Group A) copies of the last page of the text, and ask them to leave the room for their discussion. Group B stays behind in the classroom.

2 Play them the end of the recording, but do not give them copies of the text.

3 Then bring the two groups together. Each student from Group A should find a partner from Group B. They work in pairs: the students from Group B try to reconstruct as much as they can recall of the episode from their listening. The students from Group A compare their partners' oral summaries with the written text.

4.9 Listening: word recognition

LEVEL **Intermediate to advanced**

TIME **15 minutes**

PREPARATION Select a recorded passage of dialogue from a play, novel, or short story. The passage should contain words or expressions which your students may have difficulty in identifying (in speech). For instance, words which are similar in sound or meaning, such as:

genius/genie	*doom/dome*
guilt/gilt	*flawed/floored*
warn/warm	*bought/brought*
thread/threat/tread	*invincible/invisible*

IN CLASS 1 Display the words you have chosen on the board or OHP. Ask the students to copy out the list.

2 Play a recording of the passage you have chosen. (Some of the words listed under *Preparation* are drawn from Willy Russell: *Educating Rita*.)

3 Ask the students to listen to the recording and to mark with a tick (√) any of the words on their lists that they hear.

4 *Class discussion.* Which words from the list were heard on the recording?

NOTES 1 We have presented this activity in its simplest form. There is, however, a way in which you could make it more varied and challenging:

a. *Write down what you heard.* Stop the tape at certain chosen points, and ask the students to note down what they have just heard. There should be about ten stopping-points in the passage.

b. When you have played the tape through to the end, play it once again, this time without pauses. Ask the students to check their notes and, if necessary, correct them.

c. Finally, reveal the correct wording.

2 See also 4.1, 4.2, 4.3 *Focus on language* for other aspects of language which could also be tested through listening.

4.10 Writing: summaries

LEVEL   **Intermediate to advanced**

TIME   **20 – 25 minutes**

PREPARATION   This is a variation of activity 1.7 *Speculation 1*, in which the written
                       preparation was done by the teacher. Here, by contrast, it is the
                       students who do the writing.

                       1 Find three short texts which outline a situation without being too
                       explicit, that is, texts which could be interpreted in several ways
                       (for examples, see the sample texts).

                       2 Write out a short, factual explanation of what is happening in
                       each text (see *Explanations*).

IN CLASS   **1** Divide the students into groups of three. Give each group one of
                       the texts you have chosen. Ask the students to discuss their texts
                       and to decide what is happening:

                       – *Who are the protagonists?*
                       – *What are they doing?*
                       – *What is going to happen?*

                       2 Ask each group to write down two possible explanations for their
                       texts (these should not be longer than five to eight lines).

                       3 When the students are nearly ready, give each group the real
                       explanation of their text, that is, the one you have already prepared
                       (see *Preparation*, step 2).

                       Ask one member of the group to write out this third explanation in
                       his or her own handwriting.

                       4 Ask each group to join up with another group which has been
                       working on a different text. The two groups exchange their written
                       explanations.

                       5 In turn, they discuss which explanation they find the most
                       plausible.

NOTES   **1** The aim of this activity is to give the students an opportunity to
                       write in English without having to answer questions on a text.
                       Here, the text provides the initial stimulus, but the students are
                       free to work on it in whatever way they choose.

                       2 Before trying out this activity, we recommend that you introduce
                       the students to some of the activities mentioned earlier in the book,
                       1.7 and 2.2 *Speculation* and 2.8 *Completing the picture*.

SOURCES   **1** John Le Carré: *The Spy Who Came in from the Cold*
                       2 Aldous Huxley: *Those Barren Leaves*
                       3 Michael Frayn: *Sweet Dreams*

SAMPLE TEXTS

1 It was cold that morning; the light mist was damp and grey, pricking the skin. The airport reminded Leamas of the war: machines, half hidden in the fog, waiting patiently for their masters; the resonant voices and their echoes, the sudden shout and the incongruous clip of a girl's heels on a stone floor; the roar of an engine that might have been at your elbow. Everywhere that air of conspiracy which generates among people who have been up since dawn a sense – of superiority almost, derived from the common experience of having seen the night disappear and the morning come.

2 It was night. Half undressed, Irene was sitting on the edge of her bed stitching away at an unfinished garment of pale pink silk. Her head was bent over her work and her thick hair hung perpendicularly down on either side, making an angle with her tilted face. The light clung richly to her bare arms and shoulders. Her face was extremely grave; the tip of her tongue appeared between her teeth. It was a difficult job.

3 A man sits in his car at the traffic-lights, waiting for them to go green. He is thirty-seven years old, with a high forehead, and thin hair that stands on end in the slightest breeze. His eyes are a little protuberant, and his lips are set in a faint smile, so that as he leans forward against the wheel, gazing straight ahead though the windscreen, he seems to be waiting for the green light with eagerness. In fact the light has been green for some time already. Howard Baker (for that is his name) is sitting in front of a green light waiting for a green light because he is thinking. He is wondering: whether he is adequately insured, whether he should kiss Rose, the wife of the man he is on his way to see.

EXPLANATIONS

1 Leamas is a spy. He is about to set off east on a dangerous mission. He has just left his girl-friend, Liz, who does not know about his espionage activities. He is feeling nervous, because he is carrying a false passport, and almost no money. ('What about money?' Leamas asked. 'You won't need any. It's on the firm.')

2 Irene is staying with her aunt, Mrs Aldwinkle, in a *palazzo* in Rome. At the moment she is embroidering her nightdress (that is the 'difficult job'). She feels slightly ashamed of spending so much time on her clothes when she could be doing something more 'useful'. Her aunt would not approve of this. Her thoughts are preoccupied with Lord Hovenden, the man she expects to marry.

3 Howard Baker is a 'modestly successful' architect. Here, he is dreaming at the traffic lights; when he stops dreaming, he starts his car, runs through the red light, and is killed. He then goes to heaven, which he discovers to be almost identical to the world he knew on earth, with the same 'pretty suburbs, cosy dinner parties, and concerned small-talk.'

4.11 Writing: dialogues for speculation

LEVEL Intermediate

TIME 20 – 30 minutes

PREPARATION This activity is an extension of 3.2 *Creating situations from dialogue*.

You do not need to prepare any material. The preparation will be done by the students, out of class.

OUT OF CLASS 1 Ask the students to write out, at home, a short dialogue of no more than three to four exchanges on the lines of those given in the examples.

2 On a separate slip of paper, they should write out a short explanation of the dialogue.

IN CLASS 1 Ask the students to mark their initials (for example, M. B., L. J.) on the back of their dialogue slips and their explanations. Make two separate piles, one of dialogue slips, the other of explanations.

2 Tell each student to draw a paper from the pile of dialogue slips (and to check that they have not drawn their own slip!).

3 The students work in pairs. Together, they try to find explanations for their two dialogues.

4 After five to eight minutes, tell the students that they can now check their suggestions against the genuine explanations. They should look for the slip of paper bearing the matching initials (M. B., L. J., etc.) on the back.

5 *Round-up discussion.* Did any of the real explanations not match the dialogue? If not, why not? Were there any ambiguities, or errors of language?

NOTES 1 This is the last activity in the book. It is also the most open-ended. Here, the students are creating their own material, without any supervision or control. (Though there is no reason why you should not control the material after it has been produced.)

If students are to enjoy literature, and benefit from it, they must be allowed to engage with the texts, and to contribute something of their own. This is why we conclude with an open ending.

2 For further ideas on written activities connected with literature see: Maley and Duff: *Variations on a Theme* and *The Inward Ear*; Maley and Moulding: *Poem into Poem*; and also in this series, Hedge: *Writing*, Greenwood: *Class Readers*, and Morgan and Rinvolucri: *Vocabulary*.

EXAMPLES Overleaf are some examples of the types of dialogues which might be produced by the students themselves, following the model of the literary dialogues in 1.7 *Speculation 1* and 3.2 *Creating situations from dialogue* and the sample dialogues.

1 **A** Ready?
  B Not yet.
  A It's nearly eight.
  B I know, but . . . Do we have to go?
  A *You* don't have to . . . But I must.

2 **A** Did you hear that?
  B What?
  A Listen!
  B I can't hear anything.
  A Shhh. . .
  B Oh, no. Not again. It can't be!
  A It is, I'm afraid.

3 **A** Right then. Where are they?
  B Who are you talking about?
  A Come on, come on, I haven't got all day! . . . Just show me where they are.
  B But I've no idea who you're talking about. Who are you, anyway?
  A I'm from the PCB. There's my card.

EXPLANATIONS

1 A famous actress has agreed to appear in a fund-raising performance at her old school. All former pupils have been asked to bring their husbands or wives. Her husband is an airline pilot who has just returned from a transcontinental flight.

2 Two archaeologists (husband and wife) are sleeping in a hut in the jungle of New Guinea. Suspended on the roof of the hut are some skulls. Every night, the rats play with the skulls, and make them rattle.

3 An inspector from the Pest Control Board (PCB) has had a call to exterminate some hornets which have built their nest in the attic. He has come to the wrong house.

SAMPLE DIALOGUES

Below are some further dialogues from literary sources:

1 'I have something to tell you.'
'What?'
'I can't tell you over the phone.'
'Why not? Is it bad?'
'It's bad now. It might have been good once. Anyway it's nothing definite. It's more a warning than anything.'
'What can it be?'
'Use your imagination.'

(John Updike: *Marry Me*)

2 'I can see the windmill.'
'I can see the house.'
'I can see father. He's in a deckchair.'
'He's wearing his panama hat.'
'He's gone to sleep.'

'I can see your bedroom window. It's open.'
'I can see the whole, whole world.'
'I can see a bird on a currant bush. And it's a sparrow. I can see its eyes.'
'Liar!'

(Susan Hill: *Strange Meeting*)

3 'Look. Come and look.'
'Where did you get it?'
'From God. I got it from God.'
'Mary, are you all right?'
'Look.'

(Graham Swift: *Waterland*)

4 'Sometime we'll have to tell him the truth.'
'Not yet. Let's wait till summer, then we'll talk about it.'
'Why till summer?'
'To see how things go.'
'Don't you think we have a future together?'
'Sometimes I do and sometimes not.'
'When do you think so?'
'When it suddenly looks possible. I feel calm and see it that way.'

(Bernard Malamud: *A New Life*)

5 'But it's exquisite.'
'Of course it's exquisite. That's the danger.'
'The danger – I see – is because you're superstitious.'
'I'm superstitious! A crack is a crack is a crack – and an omen's an omen.'
'You'd be afraid – for your happiness?'
'For my happiness.'
'For your safety?'
'For my safety.'
'For your marriage?'
'For my marriage. For everything.'

(Henry James: *The Golden Bowl*)

Appendix

Ten generative procedures for developing language activities

It has frequently been our experience when presenting new techniques or materials to teachers that they tend to respond to the specific piece of material/technique and to attempt to relate it in a direct way to the classes they teach. ('That wouldn't work with my Class 4. It's too difficult.') This tendency is, of course, wholly natural but it does not help teachers to see beyond the specific example to the generalizable procedure which lies behind it.

By treating such activities as one-off specific instances, teachers risk being swamped in the flood of new ideas and materials which pour relentlessly from the educational presses. They also fail to develop principled and generative procedures for producing their own materials and activities in an effective and economical way.

The intention of this appendix is to show what lies behind the kinds of activity advocated in this book. We hope that this will provide the teacher with a useful tool-kit for generating his or her own materials. Once the principle behind the activity-type has been grasped, it can be applied to almost any specific text.

We wish to acknowledge the work of Christina Grieser-Kindel and Edgar Otten at the University of Cologne in helping us to clarify our own ideas. In 1988 Alan Maley gave a presentation entitled 'Twenty Things to do with Texts' at the IATEFL Conference in Edinburgh (see *Bell Academic Report: Bell at IATEFL 1988*). However, it was Christina Grieser-Kindel's presentation at the British Council Oxford Conference on Teaching Literature Overseas in April 1989, entitled 'Six Discovery Methods for Developing Language-based, Student-centred Activities' which brought about a full recognition of the power, economy, and elegance of such procedures in the context of pre- and in-service teacher training.

Here we present, not six, but ten procedures. Wherever appropriate they have been cross-referenced to the activities described earlier in this book.

1 Reconstruction

In every case the text is presented either in an incomplete or a defective form. The students' task is to restore it to its complete, original, or most plausible form. There are very many ways of doing this:

1 Jumble the words in sentences, the lines or sentences in a text, the verses in a poem, the paragraphs in an article or story, the chapters or chapter headings in a novel. Students rearrange them in an order which they can justify.
Examples in this book include:

  1.5 *Split poem*
  2.4 *Storylines 2*

2 Present only the end of a text (or the beginning or the middle, or the beginning and end without the middle). Students predict the missing part.
Examples in this book include:

  2.2 *Speculation 2*
  2.3 *Storylines 1*
  3.2 *Creating situations from dialogue*

3 Delete some or all of the punctuation, paragraphing, or verse structure. Students try to restore the original.

4 Present a poetry text laid out as a prose text (and vice versa). Students must decide whether it was originally prose or poetry and restore it to its original layout.
Examples in this book include:

  1.3 *Poetry or prose?*

5 Splice together two or more texts. These may be poems, articles, paragraphs from stories, and so on. Students have to disentangle the two texts.

6 Remove specific items from a text, leaving blanks (for content words, function words, word classes such as adjectives, linking words or phrases). This is a modified cloze procedure. Students attempt to reproduce the original or produce a plausible version.

Some versions of this activity simply present the texts with blanks. Others offer a list of possible words at the end, or a number of possible alternatives for each space.
Examples in this book include:

  2.7 *Suggesting the words*
  4.1 *Focus on language: vocabulary*
  4.2 *Focus on language: tenses*
  4.3 *Focus on language: conditional forms and if-clauses*

The most extreme version is 100 per cent cloze. In this version, students have to interrogate the teacher (or a computer) about the missing words, thus gradually reconstructing the text.

7 Delete the names of the characters who are speaking in a play, a novel, or a short story. Students have to decide who is speaking from the dialogue alone.

8 Delete the writer's comments on what the characters say or do, leaving only the dialogue or action. Students then restore authorial comment.

Examples in this book include:

1.10 *Author's comments*

2 Reduction

Students are invited to shorten the text by removing certain elements. Here are some ways of doing this:

1 Ask students to remove specific items of grammar (adjectives, adverbs, prepositional phrases, adverbial clauses, and so on.)

2 Ask them to reduce the text to zero by progressively removing one word or phrase at a time. Each resulting version has to be both grammatical and meaningful. (The shortened texts can be used as inputs to expansion activities. See 3 below.)

3 Ask students to remove authorial comment, descriptive passages, and interior monologue.

4 Students remove genre markers (that is, the items which help to identify a text as belonging to a particular genre such as a detective story, novel, newspaper report, horror story, or fairy tale).

5 Students remove a character from a novel or short story. (This activity necessarily involves some rewriting.)

3 Expansion

Students are asked to add given elements to a text. For example:

1 They add grammatical items, such as adjectives or adverbs.

2 They add descriptive passages, interior monologue, authorial comment where these are missing.

3 They add a character of a specified kind, such as a bad old woman, or a good young man. (For further ideas on this technique see Blair: *Cultural Awareness through Language*, in the *New Perspectives* series (OUP).)

4 They add an event or expand on one which is only marginal in the original text.

5 They expand a narrative text by adding what happened before it or after it.

6 They add one or more lines or verses to a poem.

7 They expand a title, an advertising slogan, or a headline into a poem, a story, a short play, or a newspaper article.

8 They add fictional footnotes or an introduction to a given text.

4 Replacement

Students remove certain elements and replace them with others. For example:

1 They change active verbs into their passive forms.

2 They replace one dominant tense by another, for example, the simple past by the historic present (use of the present tenses to describe events in the past), or past tenses by the future perfect.

3 They replace phrasal verbs by single word equivalents (and vice versa) where possible.

4 They replace as many content words as possible by their equivalent synonyms or antonyms.

5 They change the gender of characters, replacing females with males (and vice versa).

6 They change the point of view by substituting first person with third person narration (and vice versa).

7 They transform a poem or colourful prose text by replacing key images or expressions with others.

8 They transform a text from one genre into another by replacing the genre markers.

9 They change the tone of authorial comment, interior monologue, or descriptive passages (say, from optimistic or pessimistic, from detached to involved, or from enthusiastic to cynical).

5 Matching

In matching activities, the students must find correspondences between two sets of items. For example:

1 Beginnings and endings of several texts are presented. Students decide which beginnings correspond with which endings.

2 Titles or headlines are presented along with beginnings, endings, or quotations from the texts to which they belong. Students match them up.

3 Quotations are given. Students decide which characters spoke the lines.
Examples in this book include:

   2.6 *Character sketches*

4 Students match authorial comment with gaps in a text. Examples in this book include:

   1.10 *Author's comments*

5 Students match one fragment of a dialogue with another.
Examples in this book include:

   1.4 *Split exchanges*

6 Students match a title, quotation, or extract from a text with a picture. (They might ask and answer: Which picture would make the best illustration for a poem, or a book cover? for example.)

7 Chapter headings plus the overall titles of several novels are given along with outlines of the plots. Students match the two.

8 Students match descriptive words with a character in the text.
Examples in this book include:

   1.6 *Word portraits*

9 Students match 'mystery' texts with possible explanations. Examples in this book include:

   1.7 *Speculation 1*

10 Students match texts with musical extracts.

6 Media transfer

This involves the transfer of information in a text from one medium or format into another. For example:

1 Information from texts is transferred into some visual representation. For example, charts, maps, diagrams, flow-charts, tables, photographic shots, sketches of characters or settings, and so on. The information transferred can be pre-selected to refer to characters, plot, theme, vocabulary (key words), and so on. (For further ideas see Rinvolucri and Morgan: *Vocabulary*, also in this series.)
Examples in this book include:

   3.1 *Picture stories*
   3.5 *Discussion topics 2: observation*

2 Students use the information on characters or plot to prepare advertisements, book covers, posters, and collages. (For further ideas on visuals see Maley, Duff, and Grellet: *The Mind's Eye*.)

3 Using information from the text, students make up 'wanted' posters, obituaries, medical reports, or diaries for characters. (See Hedge: *Writing*, also in this series.)

4 Students transform one kind of text into another. For example, a short newspaper article into a poem (and vice versa), an internal monologue into a letter (and vice versa), an extract from a play into a narrative text (and vice versa), a narrative text into a film script or radio play, and so on.
Examples in this book include:

   3.3 *Screen adaptation*
   3.7 *Discussion topics 4: sound and silence*

5 Written text is transformed into spoken text through oral performance, using a variety of techniques such as choral and solo speaking, part speaking, modulation of pace, volume, and expression. (For further ideas on the group performance of texts see Maley and Duff: *The Inward Ear*. A very useful source of ideas on the subject of media transfer is Greenwood: *Class Readers*, also in this series.)

7 Selection

Students are asked to make a choice according to some specific criterion or purpose. For example:

1 Students decide which of a number of opening lines are from poems and which from prose texts. Examples in this book include:

   1.1 *Opening lines*

2 Several possible paraphrases of a text are presented. Students decide which one most accurately conveys the meaning of the original.

3 Students comb through a text looking for a short quotation which could serve as a title for the whole text.

4 Students look at dialogue spoken by a character and choose a quotation which best sums up that character's personality.

5 Students are offered a number of texts and must decide which would be most suitable for some specified purpose. They would look at such questions as: Which one could best be set to music? Which one would be best for display in the Underground? Which would be most suitable for a teenage magazine? Which would be easiest to translate? Which would be most suitable for radio broadcasting?
Examples in this book include:

> 1.8 *Personal choice*
> 3.8 *Discussion topics 5: the Underground*

6 Several texts are presented as entries to a competition (along with the rules for the competition). Students decide which text is the winner. They need to justify their choice.

7 Students decide which of a series of extracts come from literary and which from non-literary sources.
Examples in this book include:

> 1.2 *Sources*

8 Students are presented with several sets of texts with three extracts per set. They decide which text in each set is the 'odd man out' and why.
Examples in this book include:

> 1.9 *Odd man out*

8 Ranking

In ranking activities, the students have to decide upon an ordering of texts or items from most to least suitable for a given purpose. For example:

1 For any given series of texts, students might be asked to rank the passages in order from:
– most like 'normal' English to least like it
– most to least formal
– most to least literary
– most to least contemporary language
– richest to poorest vocabulary load
– most to least grammatically complex
– most to least personal
– easiest to most difficult to understand
– most to least interesting.

2 More specific criteria could also be set. For example:

Of any given set of texts which would be most/least suitable
- for inclusion in a woman's magazine?
- for a Sunday colour supplement?
- as a piece for broadcasting?
- for use as part of a political speech?
  etc.

9 Comparison and contrast

Normally students would be given two texts in parallel, usually on a related topic or theme. They then note points of similarity and difference between the two. For example:

1 Using two newspaper articles (or other texts such as diary entries) covering an identical event, the students:

- say which text uses the more emotive (or colourful) language
- compare the average length of words (or sentences) in each text
- decide which text shows bias.

2 Using two poems, the students think about and discuss:

- which words are common to both poems
- which words in one poem have equivalences (synonyms or paraphrases) in the other
- which ideas or images occur in both poems, and which in only one
- what rhyming patterns there are in each poem, and whether they are the same
- whether the lines (or verses) in each are the same length
- which poem leaves a clearer visual impression
- which one is more pleasant to listen to
- which is easier to understand (which words, phrases, or lines are difficult to understand in either poem)
- which they prefer, and why.

Examples in this book include:

> 2.5 *Matching texts*

3 Students compare their own versions of a text with the original. Examples in this book include:

> 3.6 *Discussion topics 3: memories*

10 Analysing

This involves putting a text or part of a text under the microscope in some way. This may range from some very mechanical procedures like counting words to the more sophisticated evaluation of the effects of words. Here are a few examples:

1 Students make various kinds of counts through a text:

- the number of definite versus indefinite articles
- the number of nouns with adjectives compared with the number without

- the number of active versus passive forms
- the number of instances of different tenses and verb forms
- the proportion of direct speech (dialogue) to indirect speech (or of dialogue to commentary)
- the number of single word verbs compared with phrasal verbs
- the average length of words (or of sentences) in the text.
- the number of subordinate clauses in the text.
  etc.

2 Analysis may also focus on particular types and instances of language. Students may be asked to:

- explore the different usages of common, everyday words in the text (such as *get, go, give, put*). How would these translate into the students' own language?
- make a list of all the formal (or informal) words in the text
- list all the synonyms or equivalences of words found in the text
- say which words in the text are neutral and which are emotive or colourful
- list all the words relating to a given topic (for example, heat) in the text
- decide which are the key words in the text (that is, the ones which convey its topic or its tone).

Examples in this book include:

  4.5 *Translation 2: everyday words*

3 The focus may also be on the characteristic collocations of words (the words which are commonly found alongside other words). For example:

- Every time a given word (say, 'home', 'the boss', 'his mother') occurs in the text, students write it down with the four words preceding it and the four words following it. These instances are arranged as a list on the page and can be subsequently analysed. A much faster way of making such concordances is to use a computer. (For further ideas on this, see Tim Johns: *Microconcord*, OUP 1990.)
- Students comb through a text looking for unusual combinations of words ('an exquisite skull', 'a hairless tomato', 'he exuded catastrophe'). They then supply more 'normal' collocations.
- In longer texts students analyse the words which typically occur in connection with particular characters (the kind of 'signature tunes' which are typical of many of Dickens' characters).

4 Various kinds of pragmatic analysis are also occasionally worthwhile. Here are two examples only:

- Students note down any utterances in which characters seem to be meaning something different from what they actually say. They then discuss what the real intentions of the characters may have been.
- Students are given a particular sentence or extract to analyse first in terms of its propositional content and then in terms of what may be inferred from it. (For example, in the sentence 'George,

kindly put the car back in the garage where you found it, before I call the police' propositionally we know that the addressee is a man, and that he has removed a car from a garage. We can also infer the relationship between the speaker and George, the reasons for his having removed it, and a number of other things.)

The examples given in the above procedures are by no means exhaustive. We hope however that they will stimulate you to generate further activities of your own using this framework of support.

Bibliography

The teaching of literature for foreign learners

Brumfit, C.J. and **Carter, S.** 1985. *Literature and Language Teaching.* Oxford: Oxford University Press.

Carter, R. and **Long, M.N.** 1987. *The Web of Words.* Cambridge: Cambridge University Press.

Collie, J. and **Slater, S.** 1987. *Literature in the Language Classroom.* Cambridge: Cambridge University Press.

Fowler, R. 1981. *Literature as Social Discourse.* London: Batsford.

Gower, R. and **Pearson, M.** 1986. *Reading Literature.* London: Longman.

Greenwood, J. 1988. *Resource Books for Teachers: Class Readers.* Oxford: Oxford University Press.

Lach-Newinsky, P. and **Seletzky, M.** 1972. *Encounters – Working With Poetry.* Bochum: Kamp.

Leech, G.N. and **Short, M.H.** 1981. *Style in Fiction.* London: Longman.

Leech, G.N. 1973. *A Linguistic Guide to English Poetry.* London: Longman.

Maley, A. and **Moulding, S.** 1985. *Poem Into Poem.* Cambridge: Cambridge University Press.

Maley, A. and **Duff, A.** 1989. *The Inward Ear.* Cambridge: Cambridge University Press.

Moody, H.L.B. 1971. *The Teaching of Literature.* London: Longman.

Morgan, J. and **Rinvolucri, M.** 1983. *Once Upon a Time: Using Stories in the Language Classroom.* Cambridge: Cambridge University Press.

Widdowson, H.G. 1975. *Stylistics and the Teaching of Literature.* London: Longman.

Collection of texts suitable for foreign learners

Adkins, A. and **Shackleton, M.** (eds.) 1980. *Recollections.* London: Edward Arnold.

Hartley, B. and **Viney, P.** (eds.) *Streamline Graded Readers.* Oxford: Oxford University Press.

Hedge, T. (ed.) *Oxford Bookworms.* Oxford: Oxford University Press.

Jackson, D. and **Pepper, D.** 1973. *Story.* (Books 1–3). Harmondsworth: Penguin Books Ltd.

Jones, E. 1987. *British Short Stories of Today.* Harmondsworth: Penguin Books Ltd.

McLean, A.C. (ed.) *Heinemann New Wave Readers.* Oxford: Heinemann.

Milne, J. (ed.) *Heinemann Guided Readers.* Oxford: Heinemann.

Oxford Progressive English Readers. Oxford: Oxford University Press.

Shackelton M. (ed.) 1985. *Double Act.* London: Edward Arnold.

Summerfield, G. (ed.) 1968. *Voices: An Anthology of Poetry*. Harmondsworth: Penguin Books Ltd.

Swan, M. (ed.) *Zero Hour and Other Modern Stories*. Cambridge: Cambridge University Press.

Taylor, P. (ed.) *A Day Saved and Other Modern Stories*. Cambridge: Cambridge University Press.

Taylor, P. (ed.) *Modern Short Stories for Students of English*. Oxford: Oxford University Press.

Articles, papers (including collections)

Barker, M.E. 1985. 'Using children's literature to teach ESL to young learners'. *English Teaching Forum* 23/1.

Boardman, R. and **Holden, S.** (eds.) 1987. *Teaching Literature*. Oxford: Modern English Publications.

Brumfit, C.J. (ed.) 1983. *Teaching Literature Overseas: Language-based Approaches*. ELT Docs. 115. Pergamon Press and The British Council.

Brumfit, C.J. 1979. *Readers for Foreign Learners of English*. Information Guide 7, The British Council.

Carter, R., Walker, R., and **Brumfit, C.J.** (eds.) 1989. *Literature and the Learner: Methological Approaches*. ELT Docs. 130. Modern English Publications in association with The British Council.

Carter, R.A. (ed.) 1982. *Language and Literature*. London: Allen & Unwin.

Gower, R. 1986. 'Can stylistic analysis help the EFL learner to read literature?' *ELT Journal*, 40/2.

Holden, S. (ed.) 1988. *Language and Literature*. Oxford: Modern English Publications.

Marshall, M. 1979. 'Love and death in Eden: teaching English literature to ESL students'. *TESOL Quarterly*, 13/3.

McConachie, J. and **Sage, H.** 'Since feeling is first: thoughts on sharing poetry in the ESOL classroom'. *English Teaching Forum*, 23/1.

Prodromou, L. 1985. 'All coherence gone: literature in EFL'. *English Teaching Forum*, 23/1.

Short, M.H. (ed.) 1988. *Reading, Analyzing and Teaching Literature*. London: Longman.

Widdowson, H.G. 1983. 'Talking shop: literature in ELT'. *ELT Journal*, 37/1.